THINKING IN CHARACTER
OR
KNOCKING ON HAMLET'S DOOR

Richard Brestoff

Thinking in Character
or
Knocking on Hamlet's Door

Richard Brestoff

Foreword by Brant Pope

Smith and Kraus   2018

A Smith and Kraus Book
177 Lyme Road, Hanover, NH 03755
editorial 603.643.6431 To Order 1.877.668.8680
www.smithandkraus.com

ISBN: 9781575259284
Library of Congress Control Number: 2018940727

Typesetting and layout by Elizabeth E. Monteleone
Cover by: Olivia F. Monteleone

For information about custom editions, special sales, education and corporate purchases, please contact Smith and Kraus at editor@smithandkraus.com or 603.643.6431.

Acknowledgements

Special thanks to Professors and colleagues Eli Simon, Phil Thompson and Andrew Borba at the University of California, Irvine for reviewing various parts of this book and either correcting misstatements of fact or noting deficiencies in explanatory passages. This book would the poorer without their contributions.

Special thanks also to Marisa Smith, Eric Kraus, Carol Boynton and Elizabeth E. Monteleone for their careful shepherding of this book into publication.

Thanks also to actor and teacher Rob Nagle for the felicitous wording of this book's subtitle.

Deepest thanks go to my wife, Melissa for reading this material and encouraging me to continue writing when my belief in it flagged. Her words inspired me.

This book is Dedicated to Melissa, to Peter Kass and to Olympia Dukakis all of whom have shown me the way. Thank you.

TABLE OF CONTENTS

FOREWORD

Only a great acting teacher would write a book on the creation of character by boldly stating, "there is no such thing as character." To this seemingly counterintuitive statement, the heads of many acting teachers will nod in agreement and so we begin Richard Brestoff's, *Thinking in Character* with one of the central contradictions of acting. An actor cannot "be somebody else," (unless they are in need of therapy) and yet the central task of the actor is to do precisely that; namely, bring the scripted character to the stage and well...... *be somebody else.* "Is there a process whereby actors can transform into characters," Brestoff asks, "without losing touch with themselves?" The answer to that question is the central business of this wonderful book and it offers the actor a specific process for creating character.

Brestoff rightly points out that very few actor training programs offer a specific curriculum or "way of working" in the creation of character. We certainly know what creating character is NOT. It is not an imitation of some other person seen in the movies or in the actor's imagination. It is not the demonstration of the Sparks notes (my character goes like THIS). Indeed, since the vast majority of scripted characters are fictional the only choice for the actor is to bring herself and her own emotional life to the service of the character and the play. But, how DOES an actor become someone else? How can (for example) a Meisner trained actor who is adept at working off the other person, create a character such as Torvald or Elizabeth Proctor or Hermione in a way that is consistent with truthfully living in an imaginary premise? How can an American actor bring a vivid and three-dimensional character to life without violating their sense of honesty and integrity?

The great value of this book is the careful way that Brestoff leads the actor through a personalization process that he calls, "embodying and **ensouling**" the character. Setting aside established text analysis methods (that he finds dry and overly intellectual), the author takes the actor through a deep investigation of the text to discover the patterns of thought displayed by the character. "By ensouling I mean the alignment of the actor with what is most important to the deepest parts of the characters they play," he states, "to their essences, to how they see and experience the world." How the character is thinking and behaving is the key information from textual analysis that allows the actor to empathize with the character and bring his genuine feeling life to the character's thoughts and behaviors.

This emphasis on behavior is particularly important because it is only through specific behavior that the audience has any idea of who the character is. In this way, the actor uses deep textual analysis to determine the emotional motives of her character and then behaves accordingly. The actor behaves and the audience (watching this specific behavior) intuitively determines character. So, back to Brestoff's point, the actor cannot PLAY character, but absolutely can create behavior that allows the watcher (the audience) to arrive at an understanding of the character. *Thinking in Character* therefore is a guidebook for helping actors do what they must do (ensoul the character) so that the audience can do what it came to do; make judgements and respond emotionally to the characters that they see in front of them.

So, the technique of thinking in character, or personalizing in character is the greatest contribution of this book to the field of actor training. Brestoff does this by creating a three-point method he calls **triangulation** to find his way into the soul of the character. Especially important is that he does this in both Realism (*Dolls' House*, *Of Mice and Men*, and *The Crucible*) and in Shakespeare (*Winter's Tale*, *Measure for Measure*, *Merchant of Venice*, *Hamlet*). In many cases he uses his own rich career as a performer and teacher to illustrate not only the successful process for ensouling a character, but also by providing examples of choices that SEEMED brilliant, but ultimately proved to be contrary to the textual clues. Most illustrative of this is his description of particular moments in *The Crucible* between John and Elizabeth Proctor where the actors struggle to triangulate the emotional location of their characters. Brestoff uses his deep textual analysis to demonstrate how an actor must sometimes discard a choice that once was revelatory but later proves to be a violation of the character. In every chapter and instance, Brestoff is teaching the reader HOW to personalize by thinking in character and HOW to deeply analyze the text for the thought patterns that reveal the humanity with which the actor can empathize. This is the book's great triumph.

In *Thinking in Character*, the actor-reader is being guided by a master teacher and given a process so that they (the actor) can do it themselves. That is a wonderful gift to the field. This book is crafted from the personal experiences of a skilled and celebrated actor who has been on Broadway, in regional theatre, and film and television. It is informed by his many other books on acting for the camera and the stage. It is also the result of many years of teaching in both undergraduate and graduate programs. Richard Brestoff is one of America's foremost acting teachers and this book is just one of the many reasons why his work is nationally and internationally recognized.

-Brant Pope
Chair of the Department of Theatre and Dance
University of Texas, Austin

PREFACE

Good thing I lost my cell phone.

I had just finished teaching my last class of the day and was heading back to my office tired and ready to go home. I packed up my computer and, as usual, checked for my wallet. It was there. I checked for my keys. They were there. As I headed out my office door, I checked for my smart phone. It wasn't there. I turned around and scanned my desk, other surfaces and the floor. It wasn't there. Some small irritation went through me. I would have to spend time searching for it and that would delay my rather long commute and the longer I delayed, the worse it would get.

Now, I often leave at least one or more of these items in a classroom or a theater or a conference room or my office and so I resigned myself to searching these spaces for the phone. This delay would mean facing major traffic jams, but I had no choice. I needed to find that phone.

I returned to my first teaching space, but it wasn't there and no one had seen it. I trudged across campus to the second teaching space, my irritation turning to alarm. I searched the second space, but did not see the device. Alarm spread to low-level panic. My pace picked up as I returned to the first space and searched it again. Still no phone. I was beginning to walk around in circles talking to myself. I knew I had it on campus, so where was it?

What about my car? I knew that wasn't possible because I had it with me when I was teaching. But I went to the car anyway. This is what we do. It wasn't there. Perhaps it had fallen out of my pocket? Yes, that was the answer! I retraced my steps staring at the ground certain I would spot it.

Kieran, a graduate acting student, saw me as I roamed around outside the second classroom and asked me what was wrong. I told him that I couldn't find my cell phone. He graciously volunteered to walk around with me searching the grounds. He asked me about all the places I had been on campus and I told him. So, we searched a café on campus where I knew I had not been that day, but we went in anyway. Naturally, it was not there and no one had turned a cell phone in. We went to the Drama office, but no one had turned in one there either.

Then Kieran asked me if I had my computer on campus. I told him that I did. He asked me if the phone I lost was an iPhone. I told him it was. He then said, "Let's try 'Find My Phone' on your computer. Do you have that enabled?" I told him I did. I had forgotten all about it in my panic.

We went to my office, I unpacked the computer, booted it up and went straight to Find My Phone in iCloud. I waited anxiously as the site loaded and then saw the computer miraculously pinpoint the location of my phone. We weren't quite sure where in the designated building the phone was, but we began searching and we found it.

Relief displaced anxiety and I raved to Kieran about the technology that allowed this to happen and I said to Kieran, "Wouldn't it be great if there was a 'Find your Character' app for actors?" It was then that I realized that what this technology had just done is what actors are always trying to do; find their character; locate their address. They want to be able to find the street their character lives on, find their house, ring their doorbell and meet them.

Perhaps someday there will be an app for this, but until that day comes my hope is that this book will, in the meantime, be helpful.

NOTE:

Please note that comments on a scene are in a normal type face while stage directions are italicized.

All quotations from Shakespeare are taken from *Shakespeare, The Complete Works.* Edited by G.B. Harrison. Harcourt, Brace & World, New York. 1952.

INTRODUCTION

The majority of actor training institutions, whether academic or private, begin their programs with encouraging emotional availability in their students. This is usually accomplished either through the repetition exercise of Sanford Meisner, the affective memory and private moment exercises of Lee Strasberg or through Uta Hagen's transference approach. There are other approaches as well, such as the Alba emotion training. What they all have in common is a focus on the genuine expression of emotion.

This work is generally known under the umbrella term, *personalization* and it is crucial. Actors are called upon to express fear, rage, tenderness, skepticism, love, attraction, humility, kindness, vulnerability, hate, frustration and the full breadth of human feeling in their work.

If personalization is taught well and the students are brave enough to take on this work, it can create emotionally responsive actors who are experiencing the roles they are playing and not merely demonstrating their understanding of them.

Student actors are hopefully encouraged not just to value their emotional lives, but to celebrate them and to use them in their acting. Again, this is critical and the present volume assumes that this phase of actor training is well in place. There is no point in moving to the study of character if the ability to personalize is not present.

The next step in actor training is known as the craft phase and is usually termed, "text analysis." Most text analysis in acting is concerned with objectives, obstacles and strategies or variations of this jargon. And while there is real value in this approach, I find much of it to be dry and overly intellectual. This is where most actors begin to become functional technicians rather than artists and some even lose their interest in acting altogether.

This occurs due to the confusion resulting from being told to follow their personal impulses during the *person-alization* phase of their training and being admonished for playing pre-conceived notions of what they think the play is about and then in the *text analysis* phase being told that personal emotions must not be played and that the pre-conceived notions of what they thought the play was about are precisely what they are now meant to conform to. This dissonance is very difficult for student actors to process and student actors in their second year of graduate training are often seen wandering the hallways in a daze.

In the final phase of training "character" is addressed. Or not. Approaches to character vary widely and there is no clear curriculum for teaching actors to characterize. Some classes will explore animal exercises with the students, some will provide trunks of dresses and shoes and hats and canes and costumes for free exploration and some will use the "centers" exercises of Michael Chekhov.

In my experience, most of these approaches fall short. At the worst, the students put on exaggerated walks or cliché accents or affect bizarre postures and the result is not character, but caricature. At best, these approaches can give the actor a feeling of being someone or something different and there is intrinsic value in that. But it is not nearly enough.

In my own graduate actor training program "character" was to be taught in our third and final year. Our teacher was a true master, working at the highest levels of artistry and inspiration. He taught some of America's finest actors over the years and I, like many others, revered him. But as class after class went by it became apparent that his powers were waning. By the end of the term we had learned very little about characterizing. There were some extraordinary extemporaneous outbursts of genius from the teacher, one nugget of which I will share in the chapter on Hamlet, but no concrete approach to character emerged.

Over the many years since receiving my MFA I have struggled with this issue. How does one become someone else? *Does* someone become someone else? I had no process, nowhere to even begin to find the character other than instinct and instinct can be very hit and miss. I read articles and books, watched videos online, initiated countless conversations with actors and teachers I admired and have finally arrived, in my later years, at an approach that provides a link between personal feeling and characterization.

What is neglected in most training is a form of text analysis focusing on *character thought patterns.* This is no longer thinking *about* the character as is usually the case in text analysis, but thinking *in* character, discovering the character's point of view, finding their take on the world, on their relationships to others and on their moment to moment emotional and behavioral adjustments to changing circumstances and then finding ourselves in there with them.

Thinking in character is not just understanding what is *said* to the character, but what is *heard* by the character. This is the shift that must take place and is the key to creating characters of depth and dimensionality.

When this work is done well it leads to the ultimate goal: *Personalizing in character.*

19

CHAPTER ONE

THE ANGLE OF LIGHT

American actors are often accused of not characterizing. Certainly praise is forthcoming for their ability to be "in the moment" and to experience real emotions on stage and on screen, but this praise is usually tempered with the caveat that, "of course they are playing themselves not the character really, but they are very good at what they do." This, despite the examples of Marlon Brando and Meryl Streep who have created a nearly unparalleled gallery of unique and believable characters on stage and on screen.

And yet it is true that many American actors stay within a limited range because they feel that taking on a character different from themselves will force them into disconnected and phony performances. Better safe than sorry seems to be the feeling and it is not an unreasonable one.

A poorly done accent, a poorly executed physicality or a tacked on attitude can indeed lead to bad acting. So, why not drop these altogether and go with something authentic and true?

In order to relieve this fear of characterizing, I will declare the following: **There is no such thing as "character."**

Now, it is certainly an odd way to begin a book on character by asserting that there is no such thing. But that is precisely where we will start.

Hamlet, Willy Loman, Hedda Gabler, Blanche DuBois, Marisol Perez, Othello, Uncle Vanya and Rose Maxson, are only words on a page. They do not actually exist. They are fictional creations of their playwrights. In other words, there is no Hamlet and there is no Marisol Perez because they are imaginary. Even characters based on actual people, living or dead, are recreations of the writer's imagination.

If in fact there *is* a Hamlet, then the role could only be played one way correctly. One actor's Hamlet would be the correct version, but another actor's Hamlet, if played differently, would not be. But if this were so, how could Richard Burton's Hamlet and Paul Scofield's Hamlet have been equally acclaimed portrayals of the part when their performances were so different? If there was such a thing as a "Hamlet" then one of them must be the right one and one of them must be the wrong one. Yet, Burton's portrayal of the character and Scofield's portrayal of the character were both entirely convincing, even legendary.

At the end of Burton's performance of Hamlet one was certain that the role not could be played in any other way. At the end of Scofield's performance of the same role one was certain that the part could not be played in any other way. There is no "Hamlet." There was Burton's Hamlet and Scofield's Hamlet. There may be your Hamlet or my Hamlet. The question is, would ours be as entirely convincing?

So then, is any approach to playing a role equally valid? If there is no Hamlet, couldn't the part be played in any way? The answer is: Possibly. But only if the clues embedded in the text are honored in a convincing way, *such* a convincing way that the audience feels, at the end of the evening, that the part could not have been played in any other way. Has one been true to the part *and* true to oneself, or is one or the other of these missing?

Actors work diligently at home and in the rehearsal room searching out who it is that they are playing and how to invest their characters with conviction, engagement and truth. But with so many bewildering possibilities in front of them, how does the actor find and execute the best choice? Often, by hunting and gathering.

Actors go down one road after another bumping into detours or "Wrong Way" signs or dead ends. They reverse course and try yet another route and they make discoveries; discoveries they might later discard as fool's gold and then they search again, hoping to find the real thing. And, with luck and intuition, they sometimes find a golden nugget or two.

But it is a haphazard process and the more they confront the reality that the human actor and the fictional character are separate and distinct, the more the frustrations mount. Actors sense that there *is* a character, but they have not yet located that character's address and they fear they may never find it. Or, even worse, they find it one day and lose it the next.

In order to gain some measure of control over this stress actors come to rehearsal either assuming some kind of character right away (putting on some character voice, or playing character attitudes and behaviors) or they simply decide that the character *is* them and play their own personal sets of behaviors, impulses and emotions.

Naturally a problem arises: If actors play the character, they often lose their grip on themselves. If the actors play themselves, they often lose their grip on the character. As one comes in, the other slips away.

As a result, what we often see in the theater are actors who look like and "perform" the character, but do not move or engage us, or believable actors who engage us, but who are unconvincing in the role.

Is there a process whereby actors can transform into character without losing touch with themselves along the way? Is there a way for actors to use themselves in the service of character?

One of the world's finest transformative actors is Meryl Streep. She is an actor renowned for her astonishing ability to "characterize" and she addresses this question directly:

> "Acting is not about being someone different.
> It's finding the similarity in what is apparently
> different, then finding myself in there."[1]

There are few actors who disappear into their characters more deeply than does Meryl Streep. Her ability to transform so often and so completely is arguably unparalleled in theatrical history and she has been rewarded for this achievement many times over. And yet, what she is saying here is that she does not disappear at all.

First, Streep acknowledges that acting a character is not about becoming someone else. She clearly understands that this is not a possibility in the literal sense.

What one *can* do is recognize the ways in which the character differs from us. This step presupposes that the actor has a good grasp of who *he* or *she* is so they can note both obvious and subtle differences between themselves and the characters they are playing.

But as they do this, they also proceed with the knowledge that these differences are only *apparent* differences. If they look closely and deeply enough, Streep is saying, they will see that the character and the actor are not so different at all.

Director Mike Nichols has identified what Streep does when she characterizes as a "subtle shift of the soul."[2] When Streep speaks of "finding myself in there," I believe this is what she is referring to. She does not vacate the premises, instead she shifts part of herself. And even a subtle shift can have seismic results.

---

1 izquotes.com.
2 Inside the Actor's Studio Season 3, Episode 7.

In this way, Streep is deeply present when she plays Margaret Thatcher or Ethel Rosenberg. Burton and Scofield are also present when they play Hamlet. As Stanislavsky quite dramatically notes:

> "...you must use your own feelings, always. Infringement of this law is tantamount to the actor murdering the character he is playing, depriving it of the pulsating, living, soul which alone gives life to a dead role."[3]

The modern cut diamond has fifty-eight facets and depending on the angle of the light falling on it only some of them reflect their brilliance back to the eye. Humans have many more facets to them than does a diamond. We call them aspects of our personality and, like the diamond, depending on the circumstances people are in and the moods they are experiencing, only *some* of their many sides are reflected back at any given time.

In playing a character an actor suppresses the parts of their psychic makeup that do not correspond to the character and highlight the aspects of themselves that *do* align with the character. In other words, the actor controls the angle of light cast on them by the character. What is reflected back is the seamless intertwining of the character's truth and the actor's truth. This is the subtle shift of the soul.

The truth is that a person cannot have another person's feeling life, only their own. In a similar way a character's emotions are not for sale or for rent or available to borrow for even a moment in time. We can sympathize, empathize and identify with others and the characters we play, but we cannot literally feel what they feel. How often have we said,

---

3 Stanislavski, An Actor's Work. Translated and edited by Jean Benedetti, NYC, NY, 2008. p.210.

"I understand" to someone only to have them reply, "You couldn't possibly understand." Of course, they are right. We couldn't possibly.

Yet, actors are charged not only with taking on their characters' emotional lives, but also their thoughts and behaviors. But in truth, no actor can have their character's emotional life no matter how hard they try.

Despite this, actors often jump into what they think are the feeling lives of their characters without recognizing that their characters may exist in a radically different emotional space and have an entirely dissimilar and unique set of reactions than they might have.

These actors have a good grasp of what is truthful for them, but have not yet found the angles of light that reflect back the specific facets of "who" they are playing. The danger is that as they rehearse they lock down certain reactions without having found what is "apparently different" in the character and *then* finding themselves in there.

Actors certainly need to be locked *in*, but they do not need to be locked *down*. locking down blinds actors to clues in the text that could align them more closely with the role. In essence, they are proceeding with neither an address nor a map.

A friend from out of town once emailed me saying that she wanted me to meet her at "the movie theater in Santa Monica." Well, there are a lot of movie theaters in Santa Monica. Which one? I didn't know if she meant a Laemmle Theater or an AMC, or a Regal Cinema. I also had no clue what street this movie theater was on. She never responded to my questions about this and we never met. How could we? No address. No map.

At some stage in the rehearsal process actors working from personal emotion run into a stumbling block and they start receiving some, or even many, mid-course corrections from the director. They are told that some of the choices they have made are not working and that the alignment between themselves and the character is off. At this point the actors usually become diffident and confused and frustrated. They feel that being emotionally connected to themselves and playing scenes honestly should be enough. And it is certainly true that emotional connection to oneself and others is of paramount, even crucial importance.

But it is not enough. Actors must understand that only a *portion* of their work has been done and realize that if they are to succeed in creating a unique human presence from words on a page, that more is demanded of them.

Now, it must be acknowledged that working from emotion first *can* work. Each person's artistic process is different and allowances should be made for that. But the downside of this is always lurking: Actors working this way risk losing their way to the character.

Another equally dangerous way to proceed in creating a role is to assume the character's physical characteristics and behaviors right from the start. Richard the Third has a limp. Blanche DuBois is always fluttery both in speech and behavior. She is sensitive and delicate. Richard III is conniving and vengeful. The actor playing Blanche wafts through the rooms blathering in a soft Southern accent seeming lost and vulnerable. Richard limps about, scowls much, and delights in his evil machinations. Hamlet is manic, he is contemplative. He shouts, he muses, he broods.

Actors are taught to be wary of such clichés, but fall into them all too easily. They are, after all, very enticing. They provide an already made wardrobe for the actor to slip into. But this wardrobe is often either too tight or too loose. Playing character becomes playing characteristics, and they are not the same thing. Personal connection and thus, depth, is absent. Facets are reflected back, but the light is artificial.

Actors cannot rely solely on personal emotions, they cannot borrow the characters' feeling lives and imitating the physical traits and behaviors of the character only leads to superficial playing. So what is an actor to do?

What actors can do is ferret out how the character *thinks*. This is the key that opens the door to character feeling and character behavior and makes it possible for actors to find themselves in what is *apparently* different and make it no difference at all.

The characters shine their light on us and we must locate which facets of ourselves are useful in reflecting it truthfully back. For instance, we must be flexible enough to shift away from our natural belief in others and towards the more paranoid aspects of ourselves if that is how the character is seeing the world. The parts of ourselves that dismiss a basic distrust of the world are not useful in playing such a character, so we dim them, background them, shift our thinking away from them so they do not ignite and we pivot to the thoughts that *do* suspect others of planning to hurt us and we let them shine through.

The question is, how do we determine which parts of ourselves to activate? In which direction do we shift the diamond?

CHAPTER TWO

ENSOULING THE PART, 1 - NORA

Surveyors use a three-point method called triangulation to determine the distance and location of a point in space. We will borrow and adapt this term in order to determine both our distance from the character and the location of their thoughts. The three-point system we will use in acting are these: Words, Circumstances and Behaviors.

If we are successful in our deployment of this approach we will then be able to find our way into the character's thoughts and into their emotions and behaviors and if we are lucky, into their souls.

We often hear the expression, "body and soul" and in acting specifically we hear the phrase, "embodying the character." But what about the "soul" part?

Embodying the character is not enough in and of itself, we also need to "ensoul" the character. It is this embodying and "ensouling" of fictional characters that is both the actor's greatest privilege and their greatest challenge.

By "ensouling" I mean the alignment of the actor with what is most important to the deepest parts of the characters they play, to their essences, to how they see and experience the world.

The simple breakdown of the process is this: "I see how the character is thinking and behaving and I can grasp the feelings that come with those thoughts and behaviors because I too have felt this same way and I have also behaved in this same way even when my circumstances were somewhat, or very, different. In this way I can empathize with the character and can bring my genuine feeling life to their thoughts and "behaviors." Simple to say, but we have to unpack this.

Imagine that characters in a fiction are phantoms that hover in the rafters of the theater or rehearsal hall. Imagine that they are bodiless and voiceless, but also know that they have the right to have their stories told, and told from their point of view. They have a right to their day in court, and know that that is what is most important to them, that it is what they crave and it is what we, the actor, can and must give to them.

The actor is their body and their voice and the actor has the responsibility to live the character's life as it felt at that time, in that moment. It is this merging of the character's inner life with the actor's, this experiencing of the part, rather than the mere demonstrating of it, that I refer to as, "ensouling."

If, at the end of a performance, the actor can look up into the rafters and see the character nodding its head, as if to say, "Yes, that is how it was for me, that is how it felt for me, you told it true," then the actor has every right to feel that he or she has embodied and ensouled the character.

If, however, the character is stoic or shaking its head, then the actor has not succeeded. If this is the case, then hopefully the actor has another night, or another take to get it right.

In order to explore this idea further, we will explore in depth a scene between Nora and Torvald Helmer from Ibsen's play, A Doll House.

Circumstances

The scene in question is near the beginning of Act Two and centers around Nora's third attempt to persuade her husband, Torvald, not to fire his employee, Niels Krogstad.

Torvald does not know that Nora has any acquaintance

with Krogstad and certainly has no idea that several years earlier Nora had secured an illegal loan from him in order to finance a trip to Italy.

The purpose of this trip was to remove the very sick Torvald from the cold climate of Norway to the far healthier climate of the Mediterranean. Nora has kept the severity of Torvald's illness from him, fearing that the news would cause him worry and anxiety and thus possibly worsen his condition. Torvald agreed to go and, after a year, fully recovered, they returned home.

Over the following years Nora has secretly made monthly payments, with interest, to Krogstad without Torvald or anyone else ever knowing.

Just before the opening of the play Torvald, a lawyer by profession, has been appointed to a new position as the manager of a bank. This means an increase in income for the family and higher prestige for him and Nora is ecstatic about it. Her secret loan from Krogstad is almost completely paid off and the Helmer family will soon enjoy a higher standard of living and her illegal loan will never be exposed.

To Nora, the future looks brighter than it has for years especially when she learns at the beginning of the play that her debtor, Krogstad, is now one of Torvald's employees. Nora has feared and disliked him for years and the loan has hung threateningly over her like the sword of Damocles. With her husband now as Krogstad's boss, she feels the power dynamic between them shifting in her favor.

Niels Krogstad, like his old friend Torvald Helmer, was also a lawyer. However, he has been unable to practice his profession for years because he was caught breaking the law himself. His crime? Forgery.

He escaped conviction on a technicality by using his skills as an attorney to exploit a loophole in the law. But while he escaped courtroom punishment, he did not escape societal shunning. His reputation was ruined, no one wanted to associate with him and he could not secure legitimate employment anywhere in town. As he says, every door was shut to him, and this is what has forced him into the business of making legally dubious loans to desperate people. One of whom being Nora Helmer.

Before the opening of the play Krogstad has finally secured a proper job. He has been hired as a clerk in a bank and can put his loan sharking days behind him. With this job, he can begin the task of rebuilding his standing in the community. But unfortunately for him, the bank in which he has so recently found employment has a new manager coming in to take over and that man is Torvald Helmer.

It turns out that Torvald and Krogstad were boyhood friends. But as adults their paths greatly diverged. Torvald became an upright citizen of the community as an employee of the local government while Krogstad has been involved in various nefarious activities which eventually land him in court facing the forgery charge.

Krogstad knows very well that Torvald dislikes him intensely and now fears that he will lose his position at the bank. In fact, Torvald strongly implies this at the beginning of the play in a scene that we do not see, but hear about.

Because Krogstad needs this job, he comes to Nora and demands that she persuade her husband to keep him employed at the bank. If she does not succeed, he tells her, he will expose both the secret and illegal loan to her husband, and also reveal to Torvald the fact that she forged her father's signature on the promissory note; the very same crime for which he was brought to trial.

Nora begins to panic. She must quickly figure out how to get Torvald to keep Krogstad employed at the bank without revealing to her husband that she has any acquaintance with him or cares about him in any way.

Her first attempt to do this comes after Helmer returns

home to see Krogstad leaving their house. He confronts Nora about Krogstad's presence and she admits that he was there to ask her to convince her husband to keep Krogstad on at the bank. Torvald is shocked that she would even entertain such a notion.

But, Nora continues to test the waters with her husband. She asks him if what Krogstad did was really such a terrible thing. He says that "yes," it was a very bad thing to forge people's names, but what was worse was the way he cleverly maneuvered his way out of taking his punishment by using lawyerly tricks. Such a man, Torvald tells her, lives his life in a deceitful way and that his lies and deceptions poison the very atmosphere of his home and are imbibed unconsciously by his children.

This stops Nora cold. She has been lying about the origin of the money for the trip to Italy for years and now is frightened that she might have been unwittingly poisoning her children. In shock, she abandons this first attempt.

Her second attempt is only referred to and is not played out as a scene in the play. Torvald says, in her third attempt, "Nora, I hope this isn't the same business from this morning." This means that earlier in the day Nora had tried again to persuade Torvald to allow Krogstad to keep his job at the bank, but we do not see this attempt on stage. It happens behind closed doors.

We now arrive at Nora's third attempt. It is later that same day. We are already part way through the scene when Torvald heads for his study. Nora stops him:

NORA

Torvald.

TORVALD

Yes.

NORA

If your little squirrel were to beg you ever so nicely for something-?

TORVALD

Well?

NORA

Would you do it?

TORVALD

First, of course, I'd need to know what it is.

NORA

The squirrel would romp around and do tricks if you'd be sweet and say yes.

TORVALD

Come on, what is it?

NORA

The lark would sing high and low in every room-

TORVALD

So what, she does that anyway.

NORA

I'd pretend I was a fairy child and dance for you in the moonlight.

TORVALD

Nora, I hope this isn't the same business from this morning.

NORA

(Coming closer.) Yes, Torvald, I beg you!

TORVALD

You really have the nerve to drag that up again.

NORA

Yes, yes, you've got to do what I say; You've got to let Krogstad keep his job at the bank.

Torvald then unwittingly gives her some ammunition saying that he understands why she is being so stubborn about this Krogstad business. It is because she is thinking of how her father was slandered by the local papers years ago and she is afraid that Krogstad, who writes a kind of gossip column himself, will write slanderous things about Torvald. Now, Nora is not actually thinking about her father, but she picks up this thread and uses it to bolster her argument.

Still, she gets nowhere:

TORVALD

What if the rumor got around that the new bank manager was letting himself be overruled by his wife-

NORA

Yes, so what?

TORVALD

Oh, of course-as long as our little rebel here gets her way-I should make myself look silly in front of my whole staff...you can bet that would come back to haunt me soon enough.

Then he finally reveals the truth:

TORVALD

Besides-there's one thing that makes it impossible to have Krogstad in the bank as long as I'm the manager.

NORA
What's that?

TORVALD
I might be able to overlook his moral failings
if I had to-

NORA
Yes, Torvald, isn't that right?

TORVALD
And I hear he's quite good at his job too. But
he was a boyhood friend of mine-one of those
stupid friendships you get into without thinking, and end up regretting later in life. I might
just as well tell you-we're on a first name basis.
And that tactless idiot makes no secret of it in
front of people. The opposite, in fact-he think
it entitles him to take a familiar tone with me,
so he's always coming out with "Hey Torvald-
Torvald can I talk to you, Torvald-" and I tell
you I find it excruciating. He'll make my life at
the bank completely intolerable.

This is the real reason that Torvald will not let Krogstad
keep his job at the bank. It is not about his forgery or about
the fact that he weaseled out of his punishment, it is that
he calls Torvald by his first name. Nora is stunned by this
admission:

NORA
Torvald, you can't be serious.

TORVALD
Oh? Why not?

NORA

No, because these are such petty things.

TORVALD

What are you saying? Petty? Do you think I'm petty?

NORA

Not at all, Torvald, and that's just the reason-

TORVALD

All right; you call me petty, I might just as well
be just that. Petty! Very well! Now we'll put a stop
to all this.

*Torvald summons the maid Helene, hands her a
letter, tells her to summon a messenger to take
it to the address on the envelope and she leaves
with the letter:*

TORVALD

So that's that, my little Miss Stubborn.

NORA

Torvald, what was that letter?

TORVALD

Krogstad's notice.

Nora has lost. Krogstad will lose his job and then reveal everything Nora has hidden fromher husband and their
lives will be ruined.

What is each character thinking, what is their behavior
and how is it different from what we might think and do in
this situation? After determining that, how do we then find

ourselves in the parts, what aspects of us align with them, what facets of ourselves need to shine through and how do we make those facets truthful and believable emotionally and behaviorally?

In other words, how do we magnetize Nora's or Torvald's souls to ours? First, there are some nagging questions that we need to answer.

Why doesn't Nora just sit Torvald down at this point and tell him the truth? Hard though it would be, this is what most of us would do. When a situation threatens to destroy our marriage or ruin our lives, we are forced to bring it out into the open because it is the only option left. But Nora doesn't so this. Why not?

Why is Torvald so upset that Krogstad calls him by his first name? Few of us will cut off all association with someone simply because he calls us by our first name. If it was that annoying to us we would simply take them aside and tell them to please stop doing this. But, Torvald does not seem to have done this. Why not? To us, Torvald's actual reason for firing Krogstad is absurd in the extreme and, yes, petty.

We also need to look at two of the words he uses in the scene to describe Nora. They are, "rebel" and "stubborn." Does he use these words just because she is continuing to argue on Krogstad's behalf, or is there also some behavior from her that justifies these words?

Nora

With regard to the first question we need to ask ourselves this: Is Nora simply afraid to tell Torvald the truth because she fears his reaction? Is she afraid that he will never forgive her, or is there some other reason? She knows how vehemently he opposes being in anyone's debt and the secret loan from Krogstad is a serious and direct violation of this edict.

Beyond that, the loan is an illegal one since a woman in that time and place could not take out a loan without her husband's written approval, and beyond that, she has committed the offense of forgery by signing her father's name as a guarantor of that loan.

These fears are reasonable answers as to why she doesn't confess to him. But these answers ignore the far more personal reason why Torvald cannot know what she has done, at least not at this time.

This deeper answer is revelatory of Nora's innermost self and is often missed by actors playing the part. This happens because they do not connect something revealed in the first scene to her subsequent behavior. It is all too easy for this to happen. So many events have gone on for Nora since that scene that the actor forgets this revelation and how it motivates so much of what Nora does in the play.

This is a crux issue for actors: Connecting *thoughts in the moment to larger thoughts revealed in earlier or later stages of the play.* It is a flaw seen in many performances. So, what is this earlier thought?

Just a few minutes into the play Nora receives a visitor. At first she doesn't recognize her, but then realizes that it is her friend, Kristine, a woman she hasn't seen for nine or ten years. As they talk about the past and get reacquainted Kristine contrasts her life with Nora's.

Kristine has had hard luck since the death of her husband. When he passed there was little to no money left for her so she had to pick up odd jobs just to sustain herself. She says, "These last three years have been like one long workday without a break." But according to Kristine, Nora's life has been very different saying to her, "…you don't know much about life's hardships yourself."

Nora bridles at this and tells her how she saved Torvald's life without ever revealing to him how seriously ill he really was and how she had to borrow money in order to make the necessary recuperative trip to Italy possible, lying to him that the money for the trip came from her father.

It is at this point that Kristine asks her a question:

KRISTINE
Didn't your husband ever find out that the money
Wasn't your father's?

NORA
Never. Papa died right after that. I thought about letting him [Papa] in on it and asking him not to say anything. But with him lying there so sick-and finally it wasn't necessary.

KRISTINE
And you've never confided in your husband?

NORA
No, for heaven's sake, how can you even imagine that? He's so strict about those things. And besides, Torvald's a man-he'd be so humiliated if he knew he owed me anything. It would even spoil our relationship; it would be the end of our beautiful, happy home.

KRISTINE
So you'll never tell him?

NORA
(Reflectively, half smiling) Yes, maybe some-day; years from now when I can't count on my looks any more. Don't laugh! I mean when Tor-vald's not as attracted to me as he is now-when my dancing and dressing-up and reciting for

> him don't interest him any more. Then it'll be
> good to have something to fall back on. Dumb,
> dumb, dumb! That'll never happen....

This is so sad and it tells us so much about her. Nora thinks that she needs some sort of insurance policy to keep Torvald in love with her after she is no longer so beautiful. When that point comes, she will then reveal everything to him about how she went to such lengths to save his life; how when the doctor told her how sick he was that she protected him from this knowledge and the subsequent worry and anxiety that such a diagnosis might cause him and how she took on secret work without him ever realizing it in order to pay off the loan balance every month for years, never spending anything on herself. When he learns these things, Nora believes, Torvald's gratefulness will reawaken his fading love for her.

What a profound and heartbreaking level of insecurity this reveals in Nora. If the sacrifices she has made in order to save Torvald's life come out now she will have no way to hold onto him in her later years. She will no longer have a way to make him love her again.

Our hearts reach out to her. We want to step in and reassure her that Torvald will love her no matter what, that true love is not about exterior values, but inner ones.

Putting this understanding of her innermost fears together with her actions in the play we begin to empathize with her, feel for her in an elemental way and her soul and ours can touch.

Yes, she is different from us, but we can also find ourselves in there with her. We intuitively understand this level of insecurity and self-doubt; we understand with her the fear of what she has to lose and in that fear we recognize ourselves and now merging with her becomes instinctive, not intellectual. We are beginning to knit together Nora's thoughts and feelings together with our own.

When Torvald tells her about the consequences of lies it shakes Nora to the core. Why?

In the famous final scene of the play one of several revelations that Nora experiences explains this. Here is what she says to Torvald:

> NORA
>
> ….When I was at home with Papa, he told me all his opinions; so of course I had the same opinions. And if I had any others, I kept them hidden, because he wouldn't have liked that. He called me his doll-child, and he played with me like I played with my dolls. Then I came to your house-

> TORVALD
>
> What kind of a way is that to describe our marriage?

> NORA
>
> *(Undisturbed.)* I mean, I went from Papa's hands into yours. You set up everything according to your taste; so of course I had the same taste, or I pretended to, I'm not really sure….

Nora has moved from her father's house to her husband's house always playing the chameleon, unquestioningly taking on the attitudes and opinions of the men providing for her because it is pleasing to them and, in doing so, finds that she can get what she wants. She is so adept at doing this that she is not even aware that she is doing it: "so of course I had the same taste, or I pretended to, I'm not really sure." She's not really sure if she is pretending. I have wondered this myself in certain situations. Have you?

Nora possesses neither Torvald's educational training nor his worldliness. So, if he tells her that a mother or a father living a life of lies poisons the atmosphere that their children breathe, she has to grapple with the fact that this might be true, and that she may be guilty of infecting her children.

An actor playing Nora may well find this idea of Torvald's utterly ridiculous. What Nora will entertain as possible, the actor may well dismiss. How then can that actor align her thoughts with Nora's?

First, the actor must recognize that the disparity between the character's way of thinking and her own actually exists and not try to ignore, dismiss or run past it. One wants to be able to stand on solid oak at all times and not on any wobbly pieces of plywood.

Second, she must consider the prospect that Torvald is right. After all, we have certainly heard the idea that if one is abused emotionally or physically growing up, that it is more likely then not that the abused will become the abuser.

If a father says he will be there for his son's recital and time after time never shows up, might not that child feel unworthy and unloved and might not that same child unconsciously repeat this same behavior with his own children? If he has learned from his father that making excuses is how you deal with life, then will he not do the same?

What about a parent who conceals what he or she does for a living because it is disreputable or illegal? Don't the children know that something is wrong, that some part of their parent's inner life is unknowable, and might they not learn to conceal themselves later on from their children?

We know that many such events in a child's life can adversely influence the way they think about the world and negatively affect their behavior in it. Parents wonder and worry nearly every day if some mistake they have made in raising their children will have some terrible lasting effect on their future happiness.

Nora's struggle with what Torvald has told her about Krogstad and his children is like this. Maybe her anxiety over finding ways to save money in order to pay off Krogstad all these years, maybe her worry that Torvald will find out about the loan has been affecting the sweet and buoyant self she tries to show to her children. Maybe the very worry and anxiety she is trying to conceal from her children is seeping through and creating in them a sense of free-floating dread.

Is Torvald so wrong? He may have a peculiar slant on it, but is this really such an unbelievable notion? We know that some new psychological finding about how the human mind works and what affects it comes out nearly every day. Maybe Nora really is a danger to her children.

Now, is it really necessary to think all of this through in order to find ourselves in what is apparently different from Nora; to find the facets of ourselves that reflect back Nora's state of mind? It is. Thinking as she does and finding the truth of that thinking in ourselves is the most critical step in embodying and ensouling her.

In thinking this through, the actor can stand on solid ground with the character because she can viscerally grasp and experience the level of uncertainty and shock Nora expresses at the end of Act 1.

The moment below occurs just after Torvald has told Nora about Krogstad's effect on his children. Torvald leaves and Nora is left alone for a moment:

NORA

(softly, after a silence) No, no! It's not true. It's not possible. It just can't be possible.

ANNE-MARIE
(In doorway, left.) The children are asking if they can come in to Mama.

NORA
No, no, no, don't let them in here with me! You stay with them Anne-Marie.

ANNE-MARIE
Very well, Ma'am.

NORA
(Pale with terror) Harm my children-! Poison my home? (short pause; she tosses her head) It's not true. It could never be true!

Serious and sickening doubt has been sown; "don't let them in here with me!" Although she tries to fight off the terror of what Torvald has told her, the instinct to protect her children from her is what leaps to the fore.

If the actor merely acts this moment, simply demonstrates her understanding of it, the result will be hollow for her and unconvincing for us. But, if the actor *experiences* this moment she will have found her way into Nora's shaken soul.

This experiencing is only possible if the character's fears and the actor's fears are inextricably linked. And this only happens when the actor genuinely aligns her thoughts with those of the character. And what is the terrifying thought that haunts Nora here? It is that Torvald may be right.

We are beginning to gain access to the way Nora sees the world, how it acts upon her and how she acts upon it, and we are beginning to feel her fears and experience her doubts. None of us is immune to the fear that we may have inadvertently psychologically damaged our children.

Yet, there another thought of hers that we have not yet explored and it is a crucial one. Nora keeps referring to "the miracle" and "…a wonderful thing." What is she referring to?

If Krogstad reveals the facts of the loan and the crime of her forgery to the authorities, then Nora is certain of the result. Her husband will step forward, shoulder the blame and take the punishment for her. He will protect the wife he loves and say that he put her up to it, that she is innocent and blameless and that he is the guilty party. This is the kind of man Nora believes her husband to be, this is the miracle: Torvald will shield her from the consequences of her actions.

And while Nora believes that this self-sacrificing heroism of Torvald's is intrinsic to his very nature, she will never allow it to manifest. How could she? Would you allow the partner you love to suffer severe and grievous consequences for something you did?

In acting we often ask, what is the character's objective, what do they want in each moment, in each scene, in this plot? If the actor believes that Nora wants to keep her secret hidden, wants to protect herself from discovery, she will play the part in a certain way and while possibly effective, she will have missed the thought that motivates Nora most profoundly.

Yes, Nora wants to keep her secret, secret. Yes, her panic seems to be about being discovered.

But, if this is the central thought guiding the behavior of the actor, that actor will then create a character primarily concerned with herself. Nora's thoughts and feelings will be focused inward and self-directed, focused on her dilemma and her desperation. She will be thinking about self-preservation and acting in ways to secure it.

But there is an outer-directed thought overriding all of these other thoughts, one that saves the actor from creating a self-absorbed character, a thought that is focused instead, outside of herself.

Once the threat is made to Nora by Krogstad in the first act, her goal, her plot objective, is to *protect her husband*. As far as she is concerned, *he* is the one in danger, not her. Nora is saving Torvald from his own heroic nature.

If all of this business comes out and there is a court trial, Torvald will convince the judge that *he* is to blame and he will go to prison in Nora's stead and she will go to any lengths to prevent this from happening. *This* is Nora's overriding fear and the impetus for her actions throughout the play. How do we know this? What proof is there? It is in the words.

Later in the scene we are examining, Torvald responds to Nora's concern about Krogstad writing a scandalous article about him:

TORVALD
….Isn't it insulting to think that I would be afraid of what some hack journalist might do for revenge?....When things get tough, I've got the courage-and the strength, you can believe it. I'm the kind of man who can take it all on himself.

NORA
(*Terrified*) What do you mean by that?

TORVALD
The whole thing, like I said.

NORA
(*Resolutely*) You'll never have to do that.

A few moments later Torvald goes to his study leaving Nora alone:

NORA
(*Distracted with fear, standing as though glued*

> *to the spot, whispering.)* He's really going to
> do it. He will do it. He'll do it in spite of every-
> thing-no, never, never in this world! Anything
> but that-escape! A way out- *(The bell rings in
> the hall.)* Dr. Rank! Anything but that! What-
> ever else happens!

Torvald means one thing in this scene, but Nora is hearing something quite different.

Torvald is reassuring Nora that he is unafraid, even
impervious to anything that Krogstad might write or imply
about him. Nora is anything but reassured.

It is critical to our ensouling of a character to recognize this
truth: That what one character *says* may not be what the other
character *hears*. Actors need to hear as their character hears.

What Nora hears is Torvald confirming to her that he
will do exactly as she expects him to do when "things get
tough;" step forward and sacrifice himself in order to protect her. This is her greatest fear and it is why the stage
direction says "*Terrified.*" If she cannot prevent it, Nora's
miracle will become her nightmare. This is the core textual
proof that justifies our choice of Nora's overall plot objective which again is, to protect her husband.

With regard to Nora's short monologue after Torvald
returns to his study there is sometimes a misunderstanding.
Some actors play this moment as if she is referring to Krogstad actually going through with his threat to expose her. They
take his "He's really going to do it" as if the "He" is Krogstad. But, clearly she is referring here to Torvald. Meaning,
Torvald really is going to step forward and take the blame for
her actions. Nora's thought here is *not* about Krogstad.

There is another connecting thought here that is often
missed. Nora is desperately looking for some solution to
her situation when the hall bell rings. She says, "Dr. Rank!"

Many actors say this as if to mean "Oh, right, Dr. Rank is coming over. I forgot." But, if that is the thought here why the exclamation point?

If we look at the thought before, we can see exactly what her thought is when she says Rank's name. She is searching for an escape, a way out of her dilemma. The bell rings and it signals the answer: "Dr. Rank!" *He* is the way out; *he* provides the escape. If she asks him for some money she can pay Krogstad off and the whole matter will disappear.

Now the exclamation point makes sense since it connects immediately to the thought before it. The question is, "how do I find a way out of this situation?" The solution, triggered by the bell is, "Dr. Rank!" The very next scene is between the two of them and in it she does indeed, ask him for "…a tremendously big favor."

Nora mistakenly believes that the whole Krogstad business will disappear if she pays off the balance of the money she owes to him. She will ask Dr. Rank for the money and she knows he will give it to her. Problem solved! For the moment at least, Nora believes that she has literally been "saved by the bell." She goes immediately into the scene with Rank intending to ask him for financial help.

Nora does everything she can to protect her husband from taking on, and suffering from, the consequences of her actions. All she wanted to do was help, and she accomplished that. Torvald recovered from a life threatening illness because of her initiative and bravery. Now, all of her loving actions are unravelling and her heroic husband will stand up for her and be caught in the crossfire. This she cannot allow.

By understanding her way of thinking about her situation our feeling life opens up to her and our empathy for her is triggered. She is caught in a trap and will do whatever it takes to free herself from it for her husband's sake. Will he do the same for her?

CHAPTER THREE

ENSOULING THE PART, 2 – TORVALD

We have examined some of the angles of light that the character of Nora throws on us and found the facets in ourselves that truthfully reflect back the thoughts and feelings contained in that light.

Now, what facets in us can truthfully align with Torvald's thoughts and feelings? How do we ensoul this character?

Unfortunately, Torvald is an easy target, easily labeled as a clueless male chauvinist. He is often played as a priggish, pompous self-centered man certain of his own superiority. Of course, if an actor sets out to "play" these characteristics then that is all his Torvald will ever be; a collection of characteristics, not a character. If we are to successfully play Torvald and not make of him a stick figure, then we will need to see the world from his point of view and allow him his humanity.

We asked earlier, why Krogstad's calling him by his first name is so abhorrent to Torvald and wondered why he doesn't simply tell Krogstad to stop doing it.

One disadvantage we have is that there is less information in the play about Torvald's history than there is about Nora's. In such an instance, we scour the play for whatever clues we can find and hope to construct a coherent and three-dimensional character from them. What are these clues and where in the text do we find them?

Very early in the 1st Act there is this dialogue between Mrs. Linde and Nora:

NORA

Did you hear about the great luck we just had?

MRS. LINDE

No, what is it?

NORA

My husband has been made manager of the Bank.

MRS. LINDE

Your husband? That is lucky!

NORA

Isn't it? The law is such a chancy business,
Especially when you won't take the ugly cases.
Torvald would never do that, of course, and I
agree with him completely.

In our world we think of the law profession as a stable and lucrative one, not a "chancy" one at all.

So, what are these "ugly cases" that Torvald refuses to accept? The play never says what they are or why Torvald turns them down, but this fact is an intriguing one and is a clue to Torvald's way of thinking about the world and his place in it.

If Torvald agrees to represent a person accused of a violent assault or of blackmail or of political opposition to the government and he wins the case then how will people perceive him?

Some of course, will see this as his job and let it go. Others however, will condemn him for enabling dangerous and disreputable people to walk the streets freely and commit more crimes against an innocent population. Torvald wants nothing whatsoever to do with cases like these because they reflect badly on him and his reputation. Are we that much different?

If you were asked to defend a serial killer or a violent political dissident, you would have to think long and hard about doing it.

William Kuntsler was an American lawyer working throughout the 1960's and 70's. He represented mobsters, radical political activists and a slew of unpopular figures including President John F. Kennedy's assassin Lee Harvey Oswald and Oswald's killer, Jack Ruby.

His other clients included members of the Black Panther Party, the Attica prison rioters and members of the American Indian Movement. He did all of this because he believed in their right to strong representation against the government.

The result? He was considered the most hated lawyer in America. If you take on these kinds of cases, then there is the potential for serious societal blowback, possible imprisonment and possible violent retaliation against you and your family. Do you want to this?

Admittedly, these are florid examples of "ugly cases," but the consequences of societal shunning still apply as far as Torvald is concerned. Torvald's thinks of it this way: "If I represent controversial people or causes, then I will be seen as sympathetic to such people and notions and become controversial myself and that will result in serious damage to my reputation, and reputation is everything." Is reputation truly as precious as Torvald makes out?

Shakespeare's Iago puts it this way to Othello:

IAGO
Good name in man and woman, dear my lord,

Is the immediate jewel of their souls.
Who steals my purse steals trash-'tis some-
thing,
nothing,
'Twas mine, 'tis his, and has been slave to thou-
sands-
But he that filches from me my good name
Robs me of that which not enriches him
And makes me poor indeed.

       -Othello, Act III, Sc. iii

Shakespeare's Mowbray says it this way to King Richard II:

MOWBRAY
….My dear lord
The purest treasure mortal times afford
Is spotless reputation….
Take honor from me and my life is done.

      -King Richard II, Act I, sc. i

Reputation is one's honor. How is a person to be trusted if their honor is suspect? One's reputation must be spotless, and Torvald's is:

TORVALD
Your father's public life was not exactly beyond reproach-but mine is. And that's how I
plan to keep it for as long as I hold my position.

Torvald's public life is beyond reproach. In the community his is an unsoiled name. It is of great interest that
Torvald singles out his "public life." His greatest concern is
what other people, the outside world, will think of him. He

makes this very clear in the final scene of the play during this exchange with Nora:

NORA
Tomorrow I'm going home-back to my old hometown, I mean. It'll be easier for me to find something to do up there.

TORVALD
You blind, inexperienced creature!

NORA
I have to try to get some experience, Torvald.

TORVALD
Abandon your home, your husband, your children? Do you have any idea what people will say?

At this catastrophic moment in their relationship Torvald's concern is for what people will say. Preserving the outward appearance of a happy marriage to the outside world is more important to him than the actual state of the marriage itself:

TORVALD
-this thing has to be covered up, whatever it costs. As for you and me, things will seem just like before.

For public consumption everything must "seem" as before, but in private, the relationship will be broken.

Torvald would rather keep up external appearances than face the humiliation of a failed marriage. Now, most of us will certainly want to maintain our privacy during marital struggles, but how can we find ourselves in Torvald here?

It repels us from him to realize how willing he is to lead a duplicitous life. He seems such a horrible man.

Would you or I really *do* this? Are we as fearful of a damaged reputation as is Torvald?

When he finds out what Krogstad might announce to the outside world Torvald's reaction is this:

TORVALD

He can still reveal everything, and if he does I'd be suspected of being an accomplice to your crimes! People might think I was behind it all, that it was my idea! And I have you to thank for all this-

Again it is, "people might think." This is the opposite of the "miracle" Nora expected of her husband. It has never crossed her mind that her brave and heroic Torvald might simply collapse under the weight of Krogstad's threat, give in to his demands and then blame *her* for it all in the bargain. But, there it is.

Now, we might be able to put Torvald's reaction down to blind panic. We are certainly not at *our* best when we are under immense and sudden pressure. But, after the initial shock Torvald makes it even worse.

When he then opens a second note from Krogstad saying that he has changed his mind and will not carry through with his threat, Torvald is ecstatic and tells Nora that he forgives her:

TORVALD

You've loved me like a wife should love her husband. You just couldn't judge how to do it.

But do you think that makes me love you any the less, because you couldn't manage by your-

self? No, no-just lean on me. I'll counsel you,
I'll direct you. I wouldn't be much of a man if
this female helplessness didn't make you doubly attractive to me....I've forgiven you Nora-I
swear I've forgiven you.

He's forgiven her? Her helplessness makes her doubly
attractive? This strikes us as craven, cowardly and patron-
izing in the extreme and we are repulsed by his depiction of
himself here as the victim. How in the world can we align
ourselves with such a man? How do we entangle our inner
life with his? Where can our souls meet?

As actors we have to face the fact that sometimes we
play less than admirable characters.

How do we do this without letting our judgement of
them affect our portrayal? *That* is the critical question. We
need to see and feel *from their point of view.* But how do
we do this when we condemn the character we are playing?

The answer lies in our most basic feelings and moti-
vations, and although these are not the first emotions that
comes to mind when thinking of Torvald Helmer, *fear* and
insecurity are the ways into his soul.

Fear, in all of its various forms is an emotion we all
share so we must examine Torvald's fears. We ask ourselves, what does this man fear most of all? He fears losing
everything he has worked so hard to achieve.

Torvald has built a reputation as a trustworthy and upright citizen of his community, a reputation that has earned
him his recent appointment as manager of the Bank. Losing
this status and subsequently losing the respect and esteem
of his peers will devastate him. So, Torvald will do what he
has to do in order to maintain his standing in society and if
he finds danger in straying too far from the straight and nar-
row, who can blame him? Torvald believes that if he follows
the rules he will be justly rewarded.

Are we really much different? This is the way most of us live our lives because it offers us the safest and least anxious pathway through life. We *want* to think of ourselves as bold and adventurous people, as heroic creatures, but mostly we play it safe. For Torvald, this approach has worked quite well. Quite well that is, until Krogstad reentered his life.

Krogstad's surprise presence as an employee at the Bank he is about to take over jeopardizes everything that Torvald has built. Krogstad is a man tainted with scandal and if it appears to others as though he is an old buddy of Torvald's, then Torvald himself becomes suspect. People may well wonder, "Why is it that our new bank manager is so friendly with such a corrupt and untrustworthy person as Krogstad?" Almost instantly, Torvald's character is thrown into question. After all, "you are judged by the company you keep," as the old saying has it.

Imagine Torvald walking into the bank and hearing his name called out with great familiarity by one of the clerks. Imagine him turning to face this friendly man and seeing Niels Krogstad; a man vilified for his under-handed behavior by the whole community. By being familiar with Torvald, it is as if Krogstad contaminates the new Bank manager with his own dubious reputation.

Guilt by association is difficult to eradicate. The best way to do it is to decisively and publicly sever the connection and that is precisely what Torvald plans to do as the play opens. But before Torvald sends the official notice of termination to Krogstad, Nora surprisingly intervenes.

And this brings us to the scene that is her third and final attempt to convince Torvald to let Krogstad keep his job.

If we are playing Torvald, do we now have enough ammunition to play him convincingly?

Have we examined thoroughly enough what is *apparently* different and then found ourselves in there?

Let's take one more look at him to see if we can solidify the empathy we are searching for.

It strikes us that this is a man who desperately needs to feel superior because he fears that he is not; this is a man who wants to see himself as a big man, but who fears that he is a small one; this is a man so insecure that he avoids any situation that might trigger the cowardice he fears will reveal itself under pressure.

These are fears and insecurities we all harbor, and although they seem to exert a particularly strong hold on Torvald, we can identify with them. Like Torvald, we fear that in a crisis we may act in ways that will expose our inadequacies. We too might not rise to the occasion, not live up to what we expect of ourselves and in this place of self-doubt and shame we can identify and empathize with Torvald because, in this respect, he is us. And in the final scene of the play we see this side of Torvald when he instantly crumples under the weight of Krogstad's threat.

We know from the play that Torvald is weak and will cave under pressure. Even Krogstad knows Torvald better than Nora does when he says to her in Act 1, "…I don't believe our bank manager has any more will power than any other married man."

We have to wonder how Torvald became the way he is. There is no answer in the script.

Perhaps the boyhood friendship he mentions with Krogstad had something to do with the construction of his fragile selfhood.

What if he was led by Krogstad into some nefarious activity and his parents found out about it? Imagine the ten or eleven-year-old Torvald overhearing his father tell his mother that their son is a cripple, a weak-willed boy who will never make much of himself in the world and that he will have to be taken care of for the rest of his life.

Eavesdropping on such a conversation at a young age would sting deeply, be hurtful, scarring and damaging. Knowing that your own father does not believe in you would be a life-long wound and you would spend the rest of your life trying to prove your father wrong. Perhaps this motivates his desire to be seen as the teacher, the learned and wise one and to be successful in the world and to cultivate respectability. In this way he can paper over the awful truth of his father's words.

This scenario comes to mind because, as a boy, I overheard my own father say this to my brother. I spent many years of my life proving my father wrong. And so I can easily find myself in Torvald.

But, is it legitimate to use such a parallel, especially when such conversation is not even alluded to in the text?

If this kind of circumstance helps to entangle Torvald's soul with mine and it fuels appropriate behaviors and emotions in me, then it is preciously useful. If, however, I use this alignment to bend the character out of shape, then it is not.

This fear of being a failure in life makes Torvald a conformist. He accepts the approved gender roles, accepts the teachings of his church and accepts the rules laid down by the arbiters of social behavior because it is safe to do so and because it assuages his fear that he is a weak-willed and small man. He does not want to put a foot wrong. This fear makes him unable to see or even to question the restraints that bind him.

Our hearts can go out to him because he is trapped by the very conformity that gives his life predictability and comfort and he cannot understand why it all isn't working. He hasn't done anything wrong, in fact he has done everything right. He is not weak. he is an admirable man.

Why then is his wife defying him? Why is Krogstad making his life miserable? Although the specifics differ, we have sometimes felt exactly this same way; that life is treating us in ways that we not deserve. The angle of light that Torvald sheds on us in this respect we can genuinely and honestly reflect back, that facet of ourselves that screams out, "Not Fair!"

Now, let's be clear. The fears that underlie Torvald's choices are only barely conscious to him. From his point of view his actions and beliefs are not those of a man run by fear, but instead are motivated by a desire to protect his wife. He needs to instruct the naïve, inexperienced and gullible Nora in the ways of the world so that she can avoid its many dangers and traps. In his mind, he does this out of love for her.

When she does not listen, he becomes exasperated and sees her as acting against her own, and his, best interests and describes her behavior as rebellious and her attitude as stubborn. We can understand the frustration of trying to help someone who refuses to be helped. This is a part of us that can also align with Torvald.

Now, lest we paint too one-sided a picture of this man we have to ask, "Does this character have any redeeming virtues?" Yes, he does.

Although he scolds Nora, he is also quick to forgive her and in his own way he truly seems to love his wife. There is a romantic moment in the play that is surprising coming from Torvald and it helps to give dimension to man so often seen as simply priggish and selfish.

In an early part of the last scene of the play Torvald confesses the following to her:

TORVALD

-do you know why, whenever I'm out at a party with you-do you know why I barely speak to you, why I keep my distance, hardly even shoot you a stolen glance? Do you know why I do that? Because I'm imagining you're my secret lover, my young, secret sweetheart, and that no one in the room guesses there's anything going on between us.

NORA

Oh yes, yes, yes-I know you're always thinking of me.

TORVALD

And when it's time to go, I place the shawl over your smooth young shoulders, around this wonderful curve of your neck-then I pretend you're my young bride, that we've come straight from the wedding, that I'm bringing you home for the first time, completely alone with you, you young, trembling, delicious-ah, I've done nothing but long for you all night....!

After a decade or so of marriage and three children, this is quite the imaginative romantic declaration! Torvald is a husband still enthralled with his wife, his desire for her still burns and he boldly tells her so. Happily, this complicates our notion of him as cold and distant and gives us a feeling for his passionate side.

This is an unexpected angle of light beaming out from him and we must catch it and reflect it truthfully back. Torvald's sexual attraction to his wife must be woven into any actor's portrayal of him.

But in the end what we see in Torvald is a mouse trying to convince himself he is a lion.

We have done a good deal of probing into the psyches of these two characters and again we ask, "Is this kind of psychologizing legitimate to engage in?" The answer once again is this: If it helps to increase our empathy with the character, then it is. If it does not serve this purpose, then it is not. After all, what we are trying to do is to see, think, feel and act from the character's point of view, not our own.

Now our task is to translate our understanding of character thought and emotion into character action.

Behavior

Behavior, along with words and thoughts, constitutes the third element we use in determining a character's location, in finding their address. At the beginning of Chapter Two we termed this procedure, *Triangulation*. It is now time to put this this technique into practice as we revisit the scene between Nora and Torvald excerpted in Chapter Two.

The following enactment of the scene is only one of *many* possible and valid ways to characterize the roles and to activate the scene. The stage directions may seem like they preexisted before the actors began rehearsals, but the exact opposite is the truth.

The stage directions were put in only *after* the actors had many exploratory rehearsals and are there because they describe what the actors did in the final performance.

The reason that this is one useful approach to the scene is because every action and reaction in it is justified by the circumstances of the play and the thought processes of the characters.

Remember, this is Nora's third and final attempt to persuade Torvald to keep Krogstad on at the Bank. We are already part way into the scene when Torvald heads for his study and Nora stops him:

> *As she speaks, Nora has a smile on her face and a gleam in her eye that feels like flirtation. Her body sways a little:*

> NORA

Torvald.

Torvald notices this good feeling coming from Nora and a smile crosses his face as he stops for a moment:

TORVALD

Yes.

She starts to cross slowly to him, her manner cute and playful. Will Nora use the promise of sexual favors to get what she wants? Our understanding of her tells us that this is certainly a tactic she is comfortable with and employs with regularity:

NORA

If your little squirrel were to beg you ever so nicely for something-?

Torvald is smiling broadly with his arms around her:

TORVALD

Well?

NORA

Would you do it?

His manner is also playful, but with a feeling of challenge in it:

TORVALD

First, of course, I'd need to know what it is.

She runs a finger gently along his cheek and puts her hands around his neck.

NORA

The squirrel would romp around and do tricks

if you'd be sweet and say yes.

He is still smiling and gives in a little:

TORVALD
Come on, what is it?

Nora leans in as if to initiate a kiss and speaks in a low voice:

NORA
The lark would sing high and low in every room-

Torvald, still playful and smiling, pulls back a little from her lips, his arms still around her and playfully challenges her:

TORVALD
So what, she does that anyway.

Nora smiles back at him and a moment later slips out of his arms. She slowly moves around behind him and knowingly whispers in his ear:

NORA
I'd pretend I was a fairy child and dance for you in the moonlight.

There is a pause as Torvald processes Nora's behavior. He is realizing that he is possibly being manipulated. His voice is somewhat neutral as he speaks:

TORVALD
Nora,

He slowly turns around to face her, his arms are on her shoulders and he speaks directly into her eyes:

TORVALD (continuing)
I hope this isn't the same business from this morning.

Nora, who can change from one mood to another instantly, gives up the playfulness and speaks desperately, putting her hands on his cheeks:

NORA
(Coming closer.) Yes, Torvald, I beg you!

Torvald is startled by this defiance. He removes her hands from his cheeks as he speaks and walks away from her, shaking his head. He seems to feel that the argument they had earlier in the morning, the one not seen in the play, had settled everything and that this whole business was finished. And now, here it is again:

TORVALD
You really have the nerve to drag that up again?

Nora's mood intensifies and erupts into a small tantrum. On the word "got" she stamps her foot on the floor. (Earlier in this chapter we asked about the words "rebel" and "stubborn" that Torvald uses to describe Nora. Now we see it not only because she is continuing to harp on the issue of Krogstad, but in her behavior as well (the foot stomp.):

NORA
Yes, yes, you've **got** to do what I say;

Why is this foot stomp a justifiable piece of behavior for the character? We glean this from something she says to Christine in the first scene of the play. In order to get Torvald to agree to the life-saving trip to Italy she tells Christine that at first she tried to "coax" him into it and when that didn't work, she then "begged and cried." Here is that same behavior. She begins this scene trying to coax him in a flirtatious way into doing her a favor and when that doesn't work she directly demands that he must do as she says. This is an intrinsic part of her behavior in critical situations, not a planned out maneuver. It comes to her naturally.

The words come out in a demanding, even petulant way:

NORA (continuing)
You've got to let Krogstad keep his job at the bank.

Torvald is taken aback at her tone. He does not speak for a moment or two. He then tries to calm her, explaining to her in a reasonable way just why it is that Krogstad cannot remain at the bank. He speaks slowly so that the words will penetrate:

TORVALD
What if the rumor got around that the new Bank manager was letting himself be overruled by his wife-

NORA
Yes, so what?

Torvald cannot believe what he is hearing:

TORVALD

Oh, of course-as long as our little rebel here gets her way-I should make myself look silly in front of my whole staff...you can bet that would come back to haunt me soon enough.

As we know, looking silly is one of Torvald's greatest fears. Nora stands her ground, not convinced by his explanation. Torvald sees this and knows he must do more to being her around.

He is now uncomfortable, because he is on the verge of revealing something personally embarrassing. He lowers his head and walks over to the hutch and buffet in their living room:

TORVALD

Besides-there's one thing that makes it impossible to have Krogstad in the bank as long as I'm the manager.

TORVALD

What's that?

TORVALD

I might be able to overlook his moral failings if I had to-

Nora is highly encouraged by this statement and brightens. This is the fair-minded and forgiving man Nora knows her husband to be. Here at last is hope:

NORA

Yes, Torvald, isn't that right?

Torvald opens a cabinet door and takes out a whiskey glass:

TORVALD
And I hear he's quite good at his job too. But…

He places the glass on the buffet just below the hutch and takes out a bottle of Scotch:

TORVALD (continuing)
…he was a boyhood friend of mine-one of those stupid friendships you get into without thinking, and…
He pours a shot into the glass:

TORVALD (continuing)
…end up regretting later in life. I might just as well tell you-

He downs a shot in one swallow and pauses, deciding. He is looking anywhere but at her. He stands there not speaking. Nora is completely still, wondering what he will say.

Nora has never seen him like this. It is as if he is about to confess to a murder or some other horrifying episode in his life. Torvald never reveals anything unflattering about himself, but he must finally tell Nora the real reason so that when she understands it, she will relent and stop defying him about Krogstad. This confession is agonizing for him. It is so private that it really is like he is confessing to a crime.

He cannot look at her. There is a long pause. Finally, he speaks in a low and confessional voice:

TORVALD (continuing)
…we're on a first name basis.…

Nora stares at him in disbelief, but he does not see it because he is looking away, unable to look her in the eyes at this vulnerable moment. There is another smaller pause before Torvald continues:

TORVALD *(continuing)*
….And that tactless idiot makes no secret of it in front of people. The opposite, in fact-he think it entitles him totake a familiar tone with me, so he's always coming out with "Hey Torvald-Torvald can I talk to you, Torvald"- and I tell you I find it excruciating. He'll make my life at the bank completely intolerable.

Here it is. The *real* reason why Torvald cannot have Krogstad as his employee. Here is the guilt by association that can destroy his reputation. It is not the crime of Krogstad's forgery or the fact that Krogstad used his lawyerly skills to avoid his just punishment or the loss of authority that Torvald will suffer if his employees think he can be overruled by his wife. No, it is the fact that this man could be perceived as his friend. A trivial reason to Nora, but a critical one to Torvald.

Nora is stunned by this admission:

NORA
Torvald, you can't be serious.

TORVALD
Oh? Why not?

Nora is so surprised; she almost laughs:

NORA
No, because these are such petty things.

He reveals a deeply sensitive matter to her and she is dismissing it by laughing at him? He feels humiliated. "Petty" is the very last thing Torvald is and to see him this way is to puncture his fundamental sense of self.

Now Torvald is in disbelief:

TORVALD
What are you saying? Petty? Do you think I'm petty?

Nora realizes that Torvald is very upset by this word and that something is going horribly wrong, so she tries to smooth the moment over by reassuring him:

NORA
Not at all, Torvald, and that's just the reason-

Torvald however, is revved up and is not about to be pacified. He cuts her off abruptly:

TORVALD
All right; you call me petty, I might just as well be just that....

Torvald goes quickly into his office and comes back into the living room holding a letter, talking all the while as he does this:

TORVALD *(continuing)*
...Petty! Very well! Now we'll put a stop to all this.

Torvald calls for the maid Helene, hands her a letter, tells her to summon a messenger to take it to the address on the envelope and she leaves with the letter:

TORVALD
So that's that, my little Miss Stubborn.

Nora has inadvertently stepped on a land mine and watches his actions and behavior with growing alarm. It is all unravelling so fast. Just a few moments before she was flirting with him.

Panic in Nora is growing rapidly:

NORA
Torvald, what was that letter?

TORVALD
Krogstad's notice.

Full panic now. The words are tumbling out:

NORA
Get it back. Torvald! There's still time. Oh, Torvald, get it back! Do it for my sake-for your own sake-for the children's sake! Listen, Torvald, do it! You don't realize what can happen to all of us.

But her words fall on deaf ears. At this point the actor playing Nora stands stock still, paralyzed and stunned at this turn of events.

*Alternatively the actor playing Nora may follow the impulse to rush out the door in an attempt to stop Helene, leaving Torvald alone on stage. Or Torvald may rush out after her, leaving the stage empty of both characters.

These variations are mentioned so that we realize that

both versions of this moment are valid.

Following spontaneous moments is a crucial part of this work. We want to be locked *in*, but not locked *down*. Later it can be determined if this alternative behavior of Nora's is more or less useful than the first choice. Variations in character behavior will present different views of the characters to the audience. In the first instance, when Nora cannot move, this tells them that she feels powerless. If she runs out after Helene this reveals that she is still trying to take action. As far as Torvald is concerned this situation is now resolved and order can be restored.

> *Torvald is calming down:*

TORVALD

Too late.

> *Nora is exhausted. She has failed. Krogstad will reveal everything and Torvald will take all the blame for her actions:*

NORA

Yes, too late.

Both of them agree that it is "too late," but for each of them there is a different meaning to this phrase. For Torvald it means that the firing of Krogstad is final and that their lives can return to normal. For Nora it means that it is too late to stop Krogstad from following through with his threat and that their normal life will now never return.

> *Nora stands stunned. Torvald walks slowly to "his" chair and sits. There is a long pause. It is quiet in the house. Torvald finally speaks and he says the next four words slowly, as if they are a sentence in and of themselves:*

TORVALD

Nora, I forgive you…

Nora stares at him, uncomprehendingly. He forgives her? For what? He notices this look and explains his thought:

TORVALD *(continuing)*

…for being so nervous about this, even though you're really insulting me….

Nora is still confused:

TORVALD *(continuing)*

Yes, you are. Isn't it insulting to think that I would be afraid of what some hack journalist might do for revenge?

Nora is still in shock:

TORVALD *(continuing)*

But I forgive you all the same, because it shows so beautifully how much you love me. That's how it should be, my own darling Nora. Come what may! When things get tough, I've got the courage-and the strength, you can believe it. I'm the kind of man who can take it all on himself.

NORA

(Terrified) What do you mean by that?

TORVALD

The whole thing, Like I said.

Nora comes over and sits next to him:

NORA

(Resolutely) You'll never have to do that, Never.

TORVALD

Good-so we'll share it, Nora, as man and wife. That's the way it should be. *(Fondling her.)* Happy now?

Nora still looks like she's seen a ghost. Torvald notices and tries to comfort her:

TORVALD *(continuing)*

Well, well, well-enough of those frightened dove's eyes. It's nothing but empty fantasy.

Nora nods her head in agreement and flashes him a loving smile. She is very good at this:

TORVALD *(continuing)*

Now you should run through your tarantella and try the tambourine. I won't hear a thing in the office, so you can make all the noise you want. *(Turning in the doorway.)* And when Rank comes, tell him where he can find me. *(He nods to her, goes to his study with his papers, and closes the door behind him.)*

Nora stands up as Torvald leaves:

NORA

(Distracted with fear, standing as though glued to the spot, whispering.)

Nora looks towards the office where Torvald just went:

NORA (continuing)
He's really going to do it. He will do it. He'll do it in spite of everything-No, never, never in this world! Anything but that-

Nora looks away from the closed office door:

NORA (continuing)
-escape! A way out- (The bell rings in the hall.) Dr. Rank!

Hope arrives in the form of Rank and now she sees a way out. As she thinks of Torvald sacrificing himself to protect her, she looks over at the office door again:

NORA (continuing)
Anything but that! Whatever else happens. *(She brushes her hands over her face, pulls herself together and goes to open the door in the hall. Dr. Rank is standing outside hanging up his fur coat.)*

The above enactment is not a prescription of how to play the scene, but rather a *des*cription of one valid way to do so. Rehearsals came first, stage directions after.

The boldest behavioral choice in the scene is Torvald's move to the hutch and buffet.

Downing a shot of Scotch is certainly not mentioned in Ibsen's stage directions. But, in rehearsal

The actor expressed a need for some liquid courage realizing that he is about to make an ignoble and embarrassing confession. This is not something that Torvald ever does. The actor's freedom in allowing this behavior to express is an admirable example of thinking as the character does and instinctively putting that thought into action.

The stakes are high in this scene for both characters and both of them behave in it as their thinking dictates, as their individual view of the consequences of losing propels them. These are real human beings grappling with serious issues, they are not symbols. Torvald is not simply a tool of an exploitative and repressive society just as Nora is not just simply a vain and superficial victim of the patriarchy. Certainly such forces are at work in the play, but "forces" do not provide playable actions for actors.

Instead, the actors are embodying and ensouling real human beings wrestling with difficult circumstances moment by moment. General themes may emerge from the action of the play, but they are byproducts of the human interactions. Without these interactions, the writing becomes an essay, not a play.

In this scene, the task of the actors was to locate the characters' addresses, to find out where they lived emotionally, intellectually, socially, physically and then to find *themselves* at that same address.

How did they accomplish this?

First, they accepted the fact that there was no such thing as a "Nora" or a "Torvald," and therefore, no single perfect way to play these characters. They accepted the idea that they do not, in fact, exist. This freed them from strictly conforming to pre-conceived notions about the characters. Instead, they accepted the idea that they personally must be present in every part they play and not absent themselves from the proceedings. It is an interesting irony that by being present in the parts we play, we seem to disappear into them. That illusion is the precious gift of good craft.

The actors then looked for areas where the characters differed from themselves in their thoughts and actions. They looked for where they would make different choices than the characters did and noted these. This presupposes, of course, many readings of the material.

Without a thorough knowledge of the circumstances and the characters, this work is nearly impossible.

Then they set about trying to find themselves in the characters by making their differences with them only *apparent* ones and not absolute ones. This is the Meryl Streep approach cited in Chapter One.

They then set their sights on ensouling the characters through the use of triangulation. By examining the words, the thoughts and the behaviors of the characters the actors began to feel for them, find empathy with them, find the places in their souls where they lined up with them.

The actors allowed the angle of light the characters cast upon them to light up the facets in them that genuinely reflected back the characters' hopes, desires, fears, thoughts and behaviors. This is ensoulment. It is not an act of disappearance. It is instead, an act of unification.

Stanislavski put it this way:

> The soul of your part will be shaped from the bits of your own living soul, your desires, yearnings, imagination. If you accomplish this creative work, then your every character will live on the stage and will possess its own individual colors.
>
> – Constantin Stanislavski

We cannot stress enough Stanislavsky's point about "individual colors. There are, and will continue to be, examples in this book that may feel constricting because they look like the way the moments "should" be played. This is far from the truth and obscures a crucial element of this work. Each moment in the examples is a way that it can be performed according to the analysis of the thoughts, feelings and behaviors of the character, but these must be enacted with the unique colors of the actor him or herself, as any other choice must also be.

Locating character is a matter of narrowing down, not adding on. The actor foregrounds the parts of themselves that correspond to the thoughts, feelings and behaviors of the character and leaves in the background the thoughts, feelings and behaviors that do not.

Yes, it is the angle of light shining on us from the characters that allows us to illuminate them, but every moment must be filled with the continuous living material of each individual actor.

If a moment in the book is described as a "pause," that is because one actor reflected the behavior of the character outward that way. No one else is bound by that pause, including the actor him or herself. Because, in another go round with the scene that same actor might, this time, rush past that moment and take the pause elsewhere. If the actor is immersed in the thoughts of the character then variations in the expression of feelings and behaviors can change.

Chapter Four

In the next three chapters we will return to the process of thinking in character, but in this one we will take a moment to allow ourselves to be inspired by examples of stunning character behavior ensouled by some of our finest actors. It is important to know what can be accomplished so that we know what the standards are and how far we can go. These actors allowed words, thoughts and emotions to manifest in such revelatory behavior that they changed the molecules in the air.

In the examples detailed below I cannot say, except in an instance or two, whether these exceptional moments were the result of actor discovery or directorial inspiration or came from other source, but they were so inspiring that they motivated other performing artists to reach for the same heights.

Of Mice and Men

In 1974 a new production of John Steinbeck's play of *Mice and Men*[iii] opened at the *Brooks Atkinson Theatre* on Broadway starring James Earl Jones as Lennie and Kevin Conway as George, with Ed Sherin directing. James Earl Jones was teaching a workshop for the NYU graduate acting program in 1974 and many of us were invited by him to a final dress rehearsal of the production.

Of Mice and Men is the story of two migrant workers who dream of someday owning their own property. They are on the move in California from one town to another because Lenny, who is developmentally backward, has been charged with rape. Although this accusation is untrue, it is true that Lenny would not let go of a woman's dress because he loved the soft feel of it.

George, who has taken on the role of Lennie's protector, leads them out of town quickly before the authorities can arrest Lennie.

The two of them wind up taking jobs as ranch hands in another town where Lenny, not knowing his own strength, unintentionally breaks the neck of the boss's son's wife and they both are forced to flee. Knowing however, that the ranch hands will eventually track them down and fearing that their revenge on Lennie will be horrific, George decides to end Lennie's life as mercifully as he can.

Lennie and George are outside by a river bank and the men chasing them can be heard in the background. The following is their final scene together:

LENNIE
I can go away. I'll go right off in the hills and find a cave if you don't want me.

GEORGE
No, I want you to stay here with me.

LENNIE
Then tell me like you done before.

GEORGE
Tell you what?

LENNIE

'Bout the other guys and about us!

GEORGE

"Guys like us got no families. They got a little stake and then they blow it in. They ain't got nobody in the world that gives a hoot in hell about 'em!"

LENNIE

"But not *us*." Tell about us now.

GEORGE

"But not us."

LENNIE

"Because..."

GEORGE

"Because I got you..."

LENNIE

"And I got you. We got each other," That's what, that gives a hoot in hell about us. *(Shouts of men again. This time closer.)*

GEORGE

(Takes off hat, shakily.) Take off your hat Lennie. The air feels fine!

LENNIE

(removes hat, lays it on the ground in front of him.) Tell how it's gonna be. *(Again sound of men. George listens.)*

GEORGE

Look across the river, Lennie, and I'll tell you-

Like you can almost see it. (Lennie turns his head, looks across river.) We gonna get a little place…"

(Reaches in side pocket, brings out Carlson's revolver. Hand and gun lie on ground behind Lennie's back. He stares at back of Lennie's head At the place where spine and skull are joined. Sounds of men's voices talking offstage.)

LENNIE
Go on! *(George raises gun, but his hand shakes and he drops his hand on to the ground.)* Go on! How's it gonna be? "We gonna get a little place…"

GEORGE
"We'll have a cow. And we'll have maybe a pig and chickens-and down the flat we'll have a little piece of alfalfa…"

LENNIE
"For the rabbits!"

GEORGE
"For the rabbits!"

LENNIE
"And I get to tend the rabbits?"

GEORGE
"And you get to tend the rabbits!"

LENNIE
"And live on the fat o' the land!"

At this point in the production George (actor, Kevin Conway) was standing just behind Lennie (actor, James

Earl Jones) with the gun in his hand:

> GEORGE
>
> Yes. Look over there, Lennie…. Like you can really see it.

Lennie keeps looking straight out, eager to see the "fat o' the land:"

> LENNIE
>
> Where?

> GEORGE
>
> Right across that river there. Can't you almost see it?

> LENNIE
>
> Where, George?

As he says this, Lennie suddenly turns his head towards George and stares straight at the barrel of the gun aimed at his head.

In all honesty up to this moment, the production had been good, but not great. We all *wanted* to be moved by Lenny's plight and George's conflicting emotions, but although there was a lump in our throat and tears were nearby, they just would not come. And then, Lennie was staring at the gun. We all held our breath and Kevin Conway froze, looking like he did not know what to do. If Lennie sees the gun the moment changes. Suddenly, Lennie knows that George is going to kill him. Will he wrestle the gun away from him, will he try to run away? We had no idea what would happen next and it looked as though Conway had no idea either.

After a stunned moment, Conway waved the gun a couple of times sideways indicating that Lennie should go back to looking out across the river. And with no change of expression Jones turned his head straight out again, looking placidly at the audience. It was as if he did not even register the gun, as if it held no more danger for him than a small stick:

>GEORGE
>
>It's over there. You keep lookin', Lennie. Just keep lookin'.

Lennie eagerly looks out with great hope:

>LENNIE
>
>I'm lookin', George. I'm lookin'.

George pulls the gun back and places it behind Jones's head.

The lump in our throats began to throb painfully and the tears started to come:

>GEORGE
>
>That's right. It's gonna be nice there. Ain't gonna be no trouble, no fights. Nobody ever gonna hurt nobody, or steal from 'em. It's gonna be-nice.

>LENNIE
>
>I can see it, George. I can see it! Right over there! I can see it! (GEORGE *fires.* LENNIE *crumples, falls behind the brush. Voices of men in the distance.*)

Many of us were crying openly as the blackout hit the stage. At that moment the director, Ed Sherin, who was sitting house center just a few rows behind us shouted out, "That's it Jimmy! That's it!"

The lights came up and Jones and Conway were still on

stage. From the house Sherin asked Jones, "Jimmy, what made you look at the gun?"

Because that was the moment. That simple turn of the head and then the turn away with no change of expression, letting us know that Lennie never felt anything other than safe with George, gun or not, that was the behavior that triggered such powerful emotions in us.

Jones replied, "The barrel caught one of the lights I guess and it was shining, so I turned to look at the shiny thing." "Well Jimmy," Sherin said, "That's the thing. That's what we've been looking for!"

Yes, it was the look at the gun and the lack of fear that made the show a searing and indelible theatrical experience. Just a look to the left and a look away. They knew something was needed, a crucial moment, but they just hadn't found it. Until this final dress rehearsal.

Why was this simple piece of behavior so powerful? You or I or James Earl Jones himself would be startled, panicky if we suddenly saw a gun pointed at our heads and would instinctively duck away from it. But not *Lennie*.

This moment movingly revealed the unconditional trust Lennie has in George. It would *never* occur to Lennie that George would do him any harm and Jones' deep connection with how Lennie thinks spontaneously took over. No panic, no fear, just George standing right next him like always.

Even the cause of the look is consistent with how Lennie behaves. Would Lennie look over at a shiny thing? Absolutely. It even seemed that Jones answered Sherin's question from Lennie's point of view. Lennie's instincts and Jones's were completely unified.

This moment was an unforgettable lesson in thinking and behaving in character. It happened in 1974 and I am writing this in October of 2017. It has been seared in my memory for forty-three years.

Measure for Measure

In 1976 Joseph Papp's Public Theater produced Shake-speare's play, *Measure for Measure* at the Delacorte Theatre in Central Park with Meryl Streep as Isabella, John Cazale as Angelo and Sam Waterston as the Duke of Vienna with John Pasquin directing.

At the beginning of the play, the Duke transfers the powers of governance to his deputy, Angelo who believes that the Duke will be in Poland. This however, is a pre-tense. The Duke never leaves Vienna at all. Instead, he disguises himself as a Friar in order to witness and evalu-ate Angelo's use of power and the reaction of the citizenry to it.

Angelo is a leading citizen of Vienna with an unstained reputation; the kind of reputation Torvald Helmer would envy. He is an austere man with puritanical beliefs and he immediately sets out to tighten the loose morals of the city. He closes the brothels and begins enforcement of an old law forbidding fornication out of wedlock, the punishment for which is death.

A young gentleman named Claudio is among the first to be arrested for violating this law and now faces execution as a result. In desperation he sends his sister, Isabella, to plead for mercy with Angelo.

Isabella is a novitiate about to take her vows as a nun when she pleads for Claudio's life to Angelo, the new and severe ruler of the city. This is his answer:

ANGELO
Be you content, fair maid,
It is the law, not I, condemn your brother.
Were he my kinsman, brother, or my son,
It should be thus with him. He must die tomorrow.

ISABELLA

Tomorrow! Oh, that's sudden! Spare him,
    spare him!
He's not prepared for death. Even for our kitchens
We kill the fowl of season. Shall we serve
    Heaven
With less respect than we do minister
To our gross selves? Good, good my lord, bethink
    you,
Who is it that hath died for this offense?
There's many have committed it.

Isabella then asks Angelo to "show some pity." This is
how he replies:

ANGELO

I show it most of all when I show justice.
For then I pity those I do not know,
Which a dismissed offense would later gall,
And do him right that, answering one foul
wrong,
Lives not to act another. Be satisfied,
Your brother dies tomorrow, be content.

Despite his unyielding words, Isabella continues to
fight, finally instructing him thus:

ISABELLA

                Go to your bosom,
Knock there, and ask your heart what it doth
    know
That's like my brother's fault. If it confess
A natural guiltiness such as is his
Let it not sound a thought upon your tongue
Against my brother's life.

This is Angelo's reply:

ANGELO
I will bethink me. Come back tomorrow.
-Act II, sc. ii

Isabella has won one more day of life for her brother, but not because her reasoning has touched Angelo's heart, it hasn't. He wants to see her again because he desires her.

When she returns the next day, he presents her with a hypothetical question:

ANGELO
Which had you rather-that the most just law
Now took your brother's life, or, to redeem him,
Give up your body to such sweet uncleanness
As she that he hath stained?

Isabella either does not understand his meaning or pretends not to and continues to present counter arguments to him. Finally, he states the depraved terms of his proposition as baldly as he can:

ANGELO
                    Redeem thy brother
By yielding up thy body to my will,
Or else he must not only die the death,
But thy unkindness shall his death draw out
To lingering sufferance. Answer me tomorrow,
Or, by the affection that now guides me most,
I'll prove a tyrant to him. As for you,
Say what you can, my false o'erweighs your
            true.   *(Exit)*

It was just after Angelo's exit and this horrific choice had been laid bare before her that Streep's body began to shake. She has a short soliloquy next, but at first no words came out. She needed to put a hand onto an archway to hold herself up, still processing the fact that her brother will not only die, but that Angelo will increase his pain and suffering by drawing it out unless she sleeps with him.

Streep's other hand went to her stomach and she began the sounds and the physical motions of vomiting. Shaken to her core, she began the soliloquy ending with this:

STREEP
            I'll to my brother.
Though he hath fall'n by propmture of the blood,
Yet hath he in him such a mind of honor
That had he twenty heads to tender down
On twenty bloody blocks. He'd yield them up
Before his sister should her body stoop
To such abhorred pollution.
Then, Isabel, live chaste, and, Brother, die.
More than our brother is our chastity.
I'll tell him yet of Angelo's request,
And fit his mind to death, for his soul's rest.
                                                -Act II, sc. iv

Streep, utterly spent and trying to catch consistent breaths and still trying to stop the nausea from consuming her body, stumbled out through the archway.

The audience was utterly silent. We had just seen a body in complete revolt, fighting off the need to retch, trying to hold itself up, attempting to speak even as waves of nausea shot through it.

We were as surprised and stunned at this as Isabella. It was as if the blood in her body was running backwards.

91

Now, it is impossible to count the thousands of words, the many different ideas that have been written and proposed explaining why it is that Isabella will not just give in to Angelo's lust and spare her brother's life. Streep made it clear in behavior.

In the very next scene, Act III, sc. i, Isabella visits her brother Claudio in his cell to prepare him for death. At first he agrees to die rather than allow his sister to sacrifice herself to rape. But as he ponders the reality of death, the fear of it changes his mind and he begs Isabella to give in to Angelo's foul demand. She adamantly and even cruelly denies him:

ISABELLA

> O you beast!
> O faithless coward! O dishonest wretch!
> Wilt though be made a man out of my vice?
> Is't not a kind of incest, to take life
> From thine own sister's shame?
> ....Die, perish! Might but my bending down
> Reprieve thee from thy fate, it should proceed.
> I'll pray a thousand prayers for thy death,
> No word to save thee.

The question that puzzles is this: Why doesn't Isabella just satisfy Angelo's desires in order to save her brother's life? This behavior is inexplicable to us and therefore needs explanation.

Scholars, critics, editors, actors, directors, students and audience members have proposed answers to this vexing problem. Isabella is supposed to be admirable in this play, the heroine, but we cannot approve of her cruelty here. Why doesn't Isabella make this sacrifice for her brother?

Isabella herself points out to Angelo that the sin of fornication out of wedlock will endanger her soul for eternity.

Her brother's death will happen only once:

> Better it were a brother died at once.
> Than that a sister, by redeeming him,
> Should die for ever. (II. iv.)

Others maintain that as a novitiate on her way to nunhood this act will destroy her goal. Some suggest that she is a strong woman who will not sacrifice herself to a brother who has betrayed her by begging her to sleep with Angelo so that he might live. Some argue that as a virgin she will not sacrifice her honor for *any* reason.

These and other arguments have been put forward over the centuries to explain Isabella's refusal and they all have their valid place in our evaluation of her motives. But putting these ideas into action, translating them into behavior, has proved elusive.

What Streep did was play the physical effects of a threatened rape. The convulsions she struggled to control told us all we needed to know. Intellectual justifications never entered our minds. We *felt* the terror not just understood it. She was not merely offended by this man's repellant lust. No, she experienced in her body and soul the sickening effect on her body of it and so did we.

When she then denounced her brother in the next scene for asking her to give in, we saw again her body react with that same sickness and understood exactly why she so adamantly rejected him. It had nothing to do with any abstract or intellectual motive, it was her *body* that seized up, her *body* that would never allow her to acquiesce, her *body* that told her it would never allow her to feel this way again whatever the "reason." Streep spewed out her denunciation of Claudio and fled the prison cell.

Years of speculation as to Isabella's seemingly cruel behavior toward her brother simply vanished, evaporated. I began to understand for the first time the terror of anyone threatened with rape. I felt physically the depth of this kind of violation *with her* and how one would do anything to avoid experiencing such a feeling again. Isabella's refusal no longer seemed like an issue at all.

Isabella no longer seemed like a religious and cold absolutist hard to identify with, but instead became a person violently struggling to exorcise a cramping nightmarish dread from her body. Nothing I had read about this character in school or afterwards prepared me for the revelation that Streep provided.

The key to what she accomplished was manifesting, in the most believable way, the *behavior* resulting from how she received Angelo's sickening proposal. It was not with anger or with defiance or with incredulousness, it was with primordial, trembling fear. This, despite the fact that Angelo (Cazale) made no attempt to accost her physically.

Streep embodied a first impulse reaction by finding herself "in there," allowed it to show and we instantly grasped the simple undeniable truth of her revulsion and the subsequent treatment of her brother.

Despite some of her words, there was nothing remotely ethical or philosophical in her reaction, it was the natural response to her circumstance and from that moment on, we empathized with Isabella.

Literary critic and author Susan Sontag notes that, "The only interesting answers are those that destroy the questions." For me, Streep's performance obliterated any questions about Isabella's refusal to help her brother. It was a visceral, powerful and inevitable reaction to violation.

Hamlet

I was lamenting to a friend about Ophelia's mad scene in Hamlet. I told him I had never seen it successfully performed. Sometimes, I told him, the Ophelia comes in with her hair down, as it is described in the play, with flowers in it wearing a diaphanous gown moving slowly, her head lolling from side to side using a "mad" voice which is usually high pitched with a wispy quality to it strewing the flowers about the stage or handing them out to the other characters.

Sometimes the Ophelia uses a voice that oscillates between the soft and feminine and the raspy low pitched voice of demon possession. Then the poor actor enacts some sort of mad behavior, often involving the flowers, and plays out the scene. It is never convincing I told my friend, and he nodded his head in agreement.

On other occasions we had both seen the "angry" Ophelia using the language to directly confront Gertrude and King Claudius. This approach we agreed, had the virtue of avoiding the "mad" Ophelia, but still was not satisfying. There really should be something very wrong with the character and anger did not really serve this requirement.

We had also seen the "sexy" Ophelia taking her cue from the bawdy material in the songs and text, sometimes removing all or most of her clothing. This wantonness is certainly justifiable, but is usually overdone and often distracting.

We also had both seen Ophelia's who alternated between wild-eyed crazy one moment, angry the next and wanton the next and back around again. We agreed that this part is a particularly problematic one for actors to play.

I told my friend about a production I had seen wherein the Ophelia came out for the mad scene trailing behind her miniature toy train cars on a string. Occasionally she would stop pulling this contraption around so that she could kneel down and adjust the cars all the while intoning the lines in a "mad" voice. Every so often she would address Gertrude vehemently.

This staging seemed like an act of desperation and was entirely ineffective. My friend was sympathetic to the actor and director noting that acting "crazy" was a very difficult challenge for anyone taking on the role of Ophelia. It was then that told me about the one production he had seen that actually made this scene work.

Ophelia came out dressed as usual, in light and flowing materials. Nothing remarkable about her except that she was carrying a scissors and was wearing a full wig.

When it came time for her to distribute the flowers and herbs named in the text (rosemary, pansies, columbine, fennel, rue and daisies) she had none of these in her hands or in her hair at all. Instead, she took the scissors and cut off pieces of her hair as if they were the foliage she named and handed each clump of hair to the other characters as if it was the herb or flower she named. Each character received their herb or flower in utter disbelief.

The madness, my friend said, was not in her voice or in the manner of her movement or in her distracted speech, but in the cutting of her hair and in her belief that her locks were in fact herbs and flowers. He said that during this simple but extraordinary display the actor spoke quite rationally with no mad voice and with no recognition of the disturbing nature of her actions. The effect he said, was electric. The whole house went quiet as each cut seemed to confirm the total dissolution of Ophelia's sanity.

Instead of trying to "act" crazy, my friend said, she just enacted deranged behavior as if it was normal. None of this was done in a dramatic way, he emphasized, and yet the result was hugely dramatic. The behavior created the perception of a psychotic break with reality, the actor had only to trust it.

I do not know if this choice was the idea of the actor or the director or the lighting designer, or the assistant stage manager. I do not know if it was arrived at after hours of rehearsal or sooner, I do not know if it came from an improvisation or from research, but none of this matters because even without seeing it myself, I know this choice works. I know because after hearing about this behavior, it is difficult for me to envision the scene unfolding in any other way. Of course, there are a myriad of choices that could work equally well or better, but when a choice makes you wonder how else it could possibly be done, then that choice is worth exploring.

This piece of behavior does not feel like the imposed, inorganic behavior with the toy trains.

No, cutting and handing out locks of one's hair and referring to them as herbs and flowers is by itself a demented act. It also has an association that comes with it; the cutting of hair is often symbolic of a depressed and erratic mind. And yet from Ophelia's warped point of view, this behavior is natural and unremarkable and because of this, the actor is freed from the task of acting "crazy."

Finding this kind of behavior, the kind that is not gimmicky or arbitrary, but folds seamlessly into the fabric of the action and is both startling and inevitable at the same time is like finding a precious gemstone. Be on the lookout for these translations of psychology into behavior, but by no means ever force them. If your focus is on embodying and ensouling the character, then discoveries like this are more likely to emerge on their own.

The Crucible

In Act Two of Arthur Miller's play, *The Crucible*, which takes place during the Salem witch trials in 1692, John Proctor is seen entering the common room of his house holding his gun. He hears his wife upstairs singing to their children, puts his gun down and tastes the stew she is making.

Proctor and his wife Elizabeth are estranged due to John's infidelity with a seventeen-year old girl named Abigail. He is trying to find his way back into her good graces, but is finding this a difficult task. He washes his hands and face as his wife enters: (The following is from an extended excerpt of the play performed for a charity and directed by the author.)

ELIZABETH
What keeps you so late? It's almost dark.

PROCTOR
I were planting far out to the forest edge.

ELIZABETH
Oh, you're done then?

PROCTOR
Aye, the farm is seeded. The boys asleep?

ELIZABETH
They will be soon. *(And she goes to the fire-place, prepares to ladle up stew in a dish.)*

PROCTOR
Pray now for a fair summer.

ELIZABETH
Aye.

PROCTOR
Are you well today?

ELIZABETH
I am. *(She brings the plate to the table, and, Indicating the food:)* It is a rabbit.

PROCTOR
(Going to the table:) Oh, is it! In Jonathan's trap?

ELIZABETH
No, she walked into the house this afternoon; I found her sittin' in the corner like she come to visit.

PROCTOR
Oh, that's a good sign walkin' in.

ELIZABETH
Pray God. It hurt my heart to strip her, poor rabbit. *(She sits and watches him taste it.)*

PROCTOR
It's well seasoned.

ELIZABETH
(Blushing with pleasure): I took great care. She's tender?

PROCTOR
Aye. *(He eats. She watches him.)* I think we'll see green fields soon. It's warm as blood beneath the clods.

ELIZABETH
That's well.

PROCTOR
(Proctor eats, then looks up.) If the crop is good I'll buy George Jacob's heifer. How would that Please you?

ELIZABETH
Aye, it would.

PROCTOR
(With a grin.) I mean to please you, Elizabeth.

ELIZABETH
(It is hard to say) I know it, John.

(He gets up, goes to her, kisses her. She receives it. With a certain disappointment, he returns to the table:

The scene begins and continues with what is often referred to as, "small talk." Sometimes small talk is needed to test the state of a frayed relationship, so they talk about the farm and the food and then, at the slightest opening, Proctor risks giving his wife a kiss. As Miller puts it, "She receives it." She does not kiss him back, but neither does she recoil. Elizabeth is still wounded by his infidelity and cannot find it in herself to let him back into her affections. Her guard still up, Proctor retreats and changes the subject:

PROCTOR
(As gently as he can:) Cider?

(Elizabeth, with a sense of reprimanding herself for having forgot;) Aye! *(She gets up and goes and pours a glass for him. He now arches his back.)* This farm's a continent when you go foot by foot droppin' seeds in it.

ELIZABETH
(Coming with the cider) It must be.

PROCTOR
(Drinks a long draught, then, putting the glass down:) You ought to bring some flowers in the house.

ELIZABETH
Oh, I forgot! I will tomorrow.

PROCTOR
It's winter in here yet. On Sunday let you come with me, and we'll walk the farm together; I never see such a load of flowers on the earth.

The stage directions from the 1980 collection of Miller plays entitled *Arthur Miller: Eight Plays* published by Nelson Doubleday of New York City in 1981 states the following:

With good feeling he goes and looks up at the sky through the open doorway.

But the actor did more than this. He bent over, reached outside the door and retrieved a bouquet of picked flowers. He turned around, gave the flowers a smell and showed them to Elizabeth.

Standing by the door, Proctor speaks with a broad and hopeful smile:

PROCTOR
Lilacs have a purple smell.

As he says the following he walks over to her encouraging her to smell them as well:

PROCTOR *(continuing)*
Lilac is the smell of nightfall, I think.

Elizabeth takes the flowers, but does not smell them. Instead, she sets them down on the table. Proctor sees this and says:

PROCTOR
Massachusetts is a beauty in the spring!

ELIZABETH
Aye it is.

There is a pause. She is watching him from the table as he stands there absorbing the night. It is as though she would speak but cannot. Instead, now, she takes up his plate and glass and fork and goes with them to the basin. Her back is turned to him. He turns and watches her. A sense of their separation rises:

PROCTOR
I think you're sad again. Are you?

Before she could answer I stopped the scene and asked the actor playing Proctor where the idea for the bouquet came from, it is certainly not in the script. His answer made this action seem obvious although I had never seen it, nor ever thought of it.

"Well," he said, "I began with the idea that Proctor is trying to get back into his wife's good graces and redeem himself for the wrong he has done to her. Then I realized from what he says that he has spent the day working in their fields, probably tilling soil and watering crops and checking on their overall condition. He has felt the soil beneath the surface and found it warm and fertile. He has walked the entire grounds and says it is a 'continent' when you go foot by foot in it and he has been overwhelmed by the sheer quantity of flowers growing on their land.

As I kind of walked the ground outside with him in my imagination it struck me that if he is trying to make amends with his wife that bringing her a bouquet of lilacs would show how much he is thinking about her and maybe break the ice."

He said that this made Proctor's comments about how she should bring some flowers into the house a great setup for surprising her with the ones he had already picked for her. "Maybe a little playful joke that they could both laugh at that would relieve some of the tension between them. I quickly realized though, from her reaction, that this was wishful thinking on my part and that my hopes for a reconciliation were not going to come true and then the wind went out of my sails."

I was impressed with his reasoning because the actor had put himself literally in the character's shoes. He imagined in detail the scene we do not see. He spent time "walking" the farm and "saw" the crops and the flowers, he spent the day with John Proctor and so the flowers were in his field of view and since he also knew and identified with Proctor's desire to get right with his wife, he put the flowers and the need together and picked a bouquet for her.

He used words, thoughts and behavior to triangulate the location of the character and found a logical and justifiable moment that served both John and Elizabeth Proctor. Now, the actor playing his wife had something new and concrete to react to.

I asked her how the moment affected her. She said, "He surprised me with it in a rehearsal and I just loved it. It was pathetic and dear all at once. Which is how I, as Elizabeth, see John anyway. As she says in the play, 'I never thought you but a good man, John-only somewhat bewildered.' Bringing me the flowers fit this description perfectly. He desperately wants to repair this relationship and naively believes that flowers will fix it, or help to fix it, but is clueless about the real depth of Elizabeth's wound. I appreciated the gesture, but my heart did not melt because of it." Her assessment of the moment felt just right for Elizabeth.

But now we have to confront an uncomfortable truth. As we continued to work it became apparent that this behavior actually distorted the scene. No matter how many different ways we tried to make this bouquet moment work, it seemed to trivialize the stakes and diminish John.

For some reason it always read as imposed, manufactured and unconvincing. More and more it felt like the kind of easy cliché that Proctor would not resort to. He is not a newlywed or a young man, but a man of experience. Miller describes him this way:

> "Proctor was a man in his middle thirties...there is evidence to suggest that he had a sharp and biting way with hypocrites. He was the kind of man-powerful of body, even tempered, and not easily led....In Proctor's presence a fool felt his foolishness instantly."

Seeing such a man as hopeful that a bouquet would break the ice with his wife belied this description and so, we dropped the moment.

One lesson we learned in our search for character behavior is this: Whether we think a moment is revelatory or something far less grand, we sometimes mistake fool's gold for the real thing. Being able to recognize and let go of an idea that does not execute well is a crucial part of both the actor's and the director's craft. So, reluctantly, we said good-bye to a perfectly justifiable idea because it violated our understanding of the character.

One other lesson we learned is that we can get caught

up in a local moment and in doing so do damage to the long range development of the character. Going back to Arthur Miller's words enabled us to see the error of our ways. It is always a good idea to go back to the play itself to check on the viability of our choices. But a part of me still wonders if this idea could still work…

The Merchant of Venice

In the summer of 2012 I played the role of Shylock in Shakespeare's *The Merchant of Venice*. In the Act IV, sc.i, set in a court of justice, Shylock insists to the "judge" (Portia in disguise) that he be allowed to take the pound of flesh from his adversary Antonio in accordance with the legal contract Shylock has made with him. In this contract, signed by both Shylock and Antonio, Shylock agrees to loan money to Antonio and take a pound of his flesh if Antonio defaults.

The "judge" hears both sides of the case and decides that according to the contract Shylock is within his rights to carry out the terms of the contract and then asks:

PORTIA
….Are there balance here to weigh
The flesh?

Shylock replies:

SHYLOCK
I have them ready.

The word "balance" here refers to a scale. Our prop was an impressive looking antique brass scale with round holders on either side of the center to hold whatever was being weighed. The scale was preset by stagehands at the beginning of the scene.

When asked about the means of weighing the pound of flesh I indicated with my arm the scale and said "I have them ready." I felt this was the appropriate manner and needed no special piece of behavior and the scene proceeded from there.

More than half way through the run of the play I happened to pick up an edition of the play that was lying around and read through this scene. It has become my habit over the years to continue to read every scene in which the character I am playing appears and then, less often, to read the whole play again. I do this because I often discover new details I have not really grasped yet in a visceral way.

In this case, I happened to glance down at a footnote at the bottom of the page and it not only changed the way I played the moment with the scale, but enabled me to find new depths in the character.

The footnote mentioned that one actor lifted the scales high above his head when he said, "I have them ready." This struck me as laughable. I thought that this was gilding the lily. To me, the scale speaks for itself and needs no such melodramatic gesture to make the point that Shylock really is going to cut a pound of Antonio's flesh from him right there in the courtroom.

But, one evening I asked myself, "why not try it?" So, that night I walked the short distance over to the scale and lifted it above my head to show it to the courtroom and said the line.

I must say that I was shocked when I heard the whole audience gasp. At first I was uncomprehending. "Why are they reacting so strongly to this?" I wondered. I realized why the actor did it now, but I did not understand the vigor of the reaction. Then it dawned on me.

That scale is the visual symbol of the sickening violence about to be acted out. All of a sudden it is real because this object will be holding and weighing out the pound of Antonio's flesh. The audience's imagination is doing the work. Needless to say, I continued to do this for the rest of the run. But not only for the sensational effect.

When the audience spontaneously reacted the way it did to the scale, I also had a spontaneous reaction to their shock. Only a second or so after their reaction I suddenly felt more vindictive towards Antonio than I ever had before and felt more evil than I was prepared for. A wave of something I will call, for want of a better phrase, "blood lust" shot through me. Their reaction to this piece of behavior connected me to the sickening thrill of revenge.

Lifting the scale now felt like a statement. A statement saying, "this act is going to take place and I am not only prepared to do it, I revel in your disgust!"

We have said that thinking in character leads to character emotion and character behavior. But this is overly schematic. Art rarely works in only one hierarchical direction. No, in this case the behavior led the way.

These examples enable us to see what others have done to translate character thought and emotion into revelatory character behavior and serve to inspire us to engage with this quest throughout our performing lives.

CHAPTER FIVE

HERMIONE, *THE WINTER'S TALE*

The plays of William Shakespeare attract and frighten actors in almost equal measure. They are attractive because they contain some of the most complex and interesting characters in all of world literature and they are frightening because of the dauntingly complex language that looms before them.

Shakespeare's plays are written in Early Modern English which is a mid-point between Old English and Modern English and was in a constant state of flux. New words were coming into existence at a rapid rate and Shakespeare coined many of them. The plays contain not only many obsolete words that require explanation, but the words are largely written in a rhythmically patterned form called, verse. In Shakespeare's case the particular rhythmic pattern is called, *iambic pentameter.* Dialogue not written in this form is called, *prose.*

Archaic wording and iambic pentameter are the first obstacles blocking access to Shakespeare's world. The words can be deciphered however, with the help of annotated footnotes and a Shakespearean lexicon.

Now, how about this pentameter issue? A "pentameter" line consists of five "feet" with a "foot" consisting of two syllables. So, a pentameter line has a total of ten syllables in it.

The "iambic" part refers to the fact that each syllable in a foot begins with an unstressed syllable followed by a stressed one. Sounds complicated doesn't it? It really isn't.

For one thing, English speakers naturally and unconsciously fall into this rhythmic pattern every day. Here is a simple example:

I think I'll go and pour myself a drink.

Count the syllables and they come out to ten. Stresses are on the second syllable of each foot:

I **think**
I'll **go**
and **pour**
my**self**
a **drink**.

So, there it is, a lovely iambic pentameter line, possibly being uttered somewhere in the English speaking world right now. It reduces some the level of anxiety when confronted with this Poetic structure to know how often English speakers naturally and easily fall into this rhythmic pattern.

Another reassuring thing to know is that Shakespeare did not always write perfect iambic pentameter lines. There are all sorts of rhythmic variations and nine and eleven syllable lines in the verse passages of his plays, with stresses on different syllables.

Still, acting students are often introduced to Shakespeare with a set of rules about all of this before they even have a chance to grasp the circumstances of the plays and the characters.

Acting students are not just readers of the plays after all, they are expected to perform them as well and an intimidating and dispiriting obstacle course of rhetorical parameters are often thrown at them before they even have a chance to get out of their chairs. This is a shame because it scares away students who might otherwise excel in this work and who decide that Shakespeare just isn't for them.

What are some of these "rules?" I have heard it said that actors in Shakespeare must not ever emphasize pronouns. This is nonsense. If a comparison is being made between two people then emphasizing the pronouns is what makes sense: "*He* did this, and *she* did that."

I have heard it said that where there is a comma you must take a short pause. Or if there is an exclamation point at the end of the sentence, you must emphasize it. It is useful to bear in mind at such times that not one play or one sentence or one word of Shakespeare's plays exists in his own hand. Let me say that again; we have no copy of any of his plays in his own hand. Every copy we have is edited by someone else.

Because the editions that exist often disagree with one another editors are needed to produce a readable, actable version. For example, they must choose between "solid," "sullied" and "sallied" for Hamlet's speech:

> "Oh, that this too too *solid* flesh would melt,
> Thaw, and resolve itself into a dew!"

Using all three words would destroy the iambic pentameter rhythm of the line, so that is probably not an option, but I have heard it done so convincingly that no one really cared if it violated the shape of the line or not.

No one knows if Shakespeare would want a period at the end of any particular sentence or a semi-colon there, or a colon, or a dash, or a comma, or anything at all. So if someone says that there is a period at the end of that line and refuses to consider that the line might work better as a question because Shakespeare put a period there, they are misleading you.

111

Some will say that all soliloquies should be taken to the audience. This is a particularly irksome rule. It is true that *some* of Shakespeare's soliloquies work best delivered to the audience, but some work best if the character feels he or she is in a private space, not being witnessed in any way.

Another rule is that there is no subtext in Shakespeare, that all thoughts, feelings and reactions are on the lines themselves. This rule is slightly more understandable because of productions that elapse over the course of five hours simply because the actors took so many unearned pauses. You do want to shout out, "GET ON WITH IT!!!"

But it is utter nonsense to eliminate reactive behavior just for the sake of speed. Sometimes, a character needs to collect him or herself, or think for a moment to puzzle something out, or to pause for a new thought to dawn.

Then there is "tradition." Puck in *A Midsummer Night's Dream* must be small and swift, running to and fro speedily to embody magical fairy fleetness and agility. Yet, the best Puck I ever saw was a man of great out-of-shape girth weighing at least two-hundred and fifty pounds. When Oberon commands Puck to scour the Earth for a particular flower Puck replies:

> I'll put a girdle round about the earth
> In forty minutes.

The actor said this looking straight out at the audience, sarcasm dripping from his mouth. The audience burst out laughing as he walked slowly and deliberately across the space and exited stage left.

A bit later in the scene he reentered stage right with the same leisurely pace holding the requested flower. Of course there was another huge laugh. But something else was also accomplished. It seemed like real magic. How could a man his size circle the earth in the few moments that he was gone? Only by magic, and suddenly he seemed endowed with a great deal of it.

But his was unusual and daring casting on the part of a very gifted director. Most of the time actors are consciously or unconsciously cast according to traditional notions that have, over the years, become normative and if you do not fit the norm, you will most likely not play the role.

Is it any wonder then that actors coming to Shakespeare feel so many crippling restraints on them? Any wonder that it feels more like they are performing in plays by Shackle-speare instead of those by Shakespeare?

Now, admittedly, some rhetorical principles can be useful, such as emphasizing and lifting the last word in a line of verse. Trying this has often yielded some interesting and useful results. But actors must keep their eyes on the prize and prioritize character thought, feeling and behavior above all else.

By using the words thoughts and behaviors of the characters, by triangulating these, we will Now examine Hermione in *The Winter's Tale*, Shylock in *The Merchant of Venice* and Hamlet in *The Tragedy of Hamlet, Prince of Denmark*.

Remember, the goal of this analysis is to embody and ensoul these characters so that the light they shine on us is truthfully reflected back, allowing for that mysterious entanglement between actor and character that distinguishes all fine acting.

The Winter's Tale

In order to locate Hermione's address, find her location and meet her there, we need not only to understand her circumstances, but also what she thinks about them and how she reacts to them.

Hermione is Queen of Sicilia and her husband Leontes is its King. The second scene of the Play takes place at their palace as Leontes tries to persuade his friend Polixenes to continue his stay at their court. Polixenes however, has already been away from his own kingdom of Bohemia for nine months and must return. Leontes is not so easily dissuaded and continues to cajole him into staying a bit longer, but he fails.

Leontes then turns to his wife, Hermione, and asks her to prevail on Polixenes and she succeeds:

LEONTES

Is he won yet?

HERMIONE

He'll stay, my Lord.

LEONTES

           At my request he would not.
Hermione, my dearest, thou never spokest
To better purpose.

HERMIONE

Never?

LEONTES

Never but once.

HERMIONE

What! Have I twice said well? When was't before?
I prithee tell me, cram's with praise, and make's
As fat as tame things. One good deed dying
        tongue-less
Slaughters a thousand waiting upon that.
Our praises are our wages. You may ride's

With one soft kiss a thousand furlongs ere
With spur we heat an acre. But to the goal.
My last good deed was to entreat his stay.
What was my first? It has an elder sister,
Or I mistake you. Oh, would her name was
        Grace!
But once before I spoke to the purpose-when?
Nay, let me have't, I long.

LEONTES

Why that was when
Three crabbéd months had soured themselves to
        death
Ere I could make thee open thy white hand
And clap thyself my love. Then didst thou utter
"I am yours forever."

HERMIONE

'Tis Grace indeed.
Why lo you now, I have spoke to the purpose twice.
The one forever earned a royal husband,
The other for some while a friend.

The literal sense of this dialogue needs parsing before
we can move forward. First, the layout on the page follows that of editor G.B. Harrison in his *Shakespeare, The
Complete Works* as does the layout of every quotation from
Shakespeare in this book (See NOTE).

The first several exchanges need no clarification. Hermione has succeeded where Leontes could not. The problem
begins with these lines from Hermione:

I prithee tell me, cram's with praise, and make's
As fat as tame things. One good deed dying

115

> tongue-less
> Slaughters a thousand waiting upon that.
> Our praises are our wages. You may ride's
> With one soft kiss a thousand furlongs ere
> With spur we heat an acre.

What does this mean? What is she literally saying? Words are a crucial part of the triangulation approach, so we must pay attention to them or we will lose the thoughts of the character:

> "Cram's with praise, and make's
> As fat as tame things."

This means, "Fill me up with praise and make me as full with them as well-fed animals are with their food:"

> One good deed dying tongue-less
> Slaughters a thousand waiting upon that.
> Our praises are our wages. You may ride's
> With one soft kiss a thousand furlongs ere
> With spur we heat an acre.

The first sentence here means, "if one good deed is not met with acknowledgement and appreciation a thousand others, which could have been in the offing, are killed off." In other words, why would anyone want to do anything wonderful for you again if you never took the time to thank them for their efforts the first time?

The second sentence is as clear and eloquent as it could be: Praises are payments. The more of them we receive, the richer we feel inside.

The third sentence needs some untangling:

You may ride's
With one soft kiss a thousand furlongs ere
With spur we heat an acre.

This means, you will go much further with adoring words (soft kiss) than you ever will with harsh ones (spur). The comparison, or antithesis, is between "kiss" and "spur."

Hermione loves to hear her husband praise her and yearns for more, "...let me have't, I long."

Leontes seems to playfully withhold his answer, but then complies with her request and tells her that the only time she spoke better was when, after three torturous months of courting and waiting she spoke these words, "I am yours forever."

This is very romantic and flirtatious once we understand the literal sense of the words. Hermione is longing to hear their love story again and he teases her for a moment or two before telling it to her. Here is a place where we can identify with her. We too love to be complimented and we also relish hearing our love story recalled to us by our mate. This winning romantic part of her can be found in our own feeling life and can easily be reflected truthfully back.

But this nice shared moment of affection is shattered in the next few moments by a sudden and shattering reversal.

Hermione moves over to Polixenes, holds his hand and chats with him. With no more provocation than this, Leontes flies into a mad rage of jealousy which begins as an aside as he watches his wife and Polixenes:

LEONTES
Too hot, too hot!
To mingle friendship far is mingling bloods.
I have tremor cordis on me. My heart dances,
But not for joy, not joy.

We must unpack words again: *tremor cordis* refers to heart palpitations, in this case caused by the extreme agitation of jealousy. In a few horrible moments he unaccountably concludes that Polixenes and Hermione are having an affair and that the child his wife is carrying is not his, but was fathered by Polixenes.

Where does this come from? Only a few seconds before Leontes was praising Hermione and flirting with her. Now, suddenly, he is drawing the most suspicious conclusions from a pleasant interaction between the two of them.

When one of his lords, Camillo, insists that there is nothing between Leontes's friend and his wife Leontes responds with extreme paranoia:

LEONTES

Is whispering nothing?
Is leaning cheek to cheek? Is meeting noses?
Kissing with inside lip? Stopping the career
Of laughter with a sigh-a note infallible
Of breaking honesty?-horsing foot on foot?
Skulking in corners? Wishing clocks more swift?
Hours, minutes? Noon, midnight? And all eyes
Blind with the pin and web, but theirs, theirs only,
That would unseen be wicked? Is this nothing?
Why, then the world and all that's in 't is nothing,
The covering sky is nothing, Bohemia nothing,
My wife is nothing, nor nothing have these nothings
If this be nothing.

CAMILO

Good my lord, be cured
Of this diseased opinion, and betimes,
For tis most dangerous.

Dangerous indeed. In this eruption of jealousy Leontes orders Camillo to murder Polixenes, forbids Hermione contact with their young son, denounces her as an adulteress and a traitor and imprisons her. While there, Hermione gives birth to the daughter that Leontes believes is Polixenes's child and orders this newborn baby girl to be "...instantly consumed with fire." Four words that describe perfectly Leontes himself. He is instantly consumed with fire and it will not burn itself out. He orders Hermione to stand trial.

A Court of Justice is the setting for the second scene in Act III. It is here that Leontes arraigns Hermione:

LEONTES
Read the indictment.

OFFICER
(Reads.) "Hermione, Queen to the worthy Leontes, King of Sicilia, thou art here accused and arraigned of high treason, in committing adultery with Polixenes, King of Bohemia, and conspiring with Camillo to take away the life of our Sovereign, Lord the King, thy royal husband."

The indictment goes on a bit further before Hermione has a chance to defend herself. But when she does Leontes remains unconvinced and threatens her with death:

LEONTES
....You had a bastard by Polixenes...so thou
Shalt feel our justice, in whose easiest passage
Look for no more than death.

Hermione responds to this threat in her next speech, a monologue which we will analyze for performance:

119

HERMIONE

Sir, spare your threats.
The bug which you would fright me with I seek.
To me can life be no commodity.
The crown and comfort of my life, your favor,
I do give lost, for I do feel it gone,
But know not how it went. My second joy
And first-fruits of my body, from his presence
I am barred as one infectious. My third comfort,
Starred most unluckily, is from my breast,
The innocent milk in it most innocent mouth,
Haled out to murder. Myself on every post
Proclaimed a strumpet, with immodest hatred
The childbed privilege denied which 'longs
To women of all fashion; lastly, hurried
Here to this place I' the open air before
I have got strength of limit. Now my liege,
Tell me what blessings I have here alive,
That I should fear to die? Therefore proceed.
But yet hear this, mistake me not, no life-
I prize it not a straw-but for mine honor,
Which I would free, if I shall be condemned
Upon surmises, all proofs sleeping else
But what your jealousies awake, I tell you
'Tis rigor and not law. Your honors all,
I do refer me to the oracle.
Apollo be my judge!

There are some words and phrases that require explanation here before we can move forward. First is the line, "To me life can be no commodity." How is the word "commodity" to be understood here? The word in this context means, "advantage." So, Hermione is saying that life itself holds no advantage for her over death.

Her "second joy" is her son who has been barred from her presence by Leontes. Her "third comfort" is the child to whom she has given birth in prison and who is destined, by Leontes' command, to be murdered. She is deprived of all of these comforts.

Her, "childbed privilege denied which 'longs to women of all fashion," refers to the privilege accorded to women of every class to recuperate and rest after childbirth. She is denied this as well.

At the end of the speech she speaks of "rigor and not law." She means that the charges against her are not the result of broken laws as there is no proof for any of them, but instead result only from Leontes' stiffness (as in rigor mortis), from his own personal inflexibility and harshness.

When she speaks of the "oracle" and "Apollo be my judge," she is referring to the fact that Leontes has sent messengers to the oracle at Delphi to verify the truth and justice of his punishments upon Hermione and Polixenes. Hermione declares here that she is content to abide by whatever the oracle decides and will accept its judgement of her innocence or guilt.

How are we to approach this monologue? If we approach it from our first emotional response it might be characterized by anger and outrage. It might go something like this:

Angrily, almost spitting it out:

HERMIONE

Sir, spare your threats.

Her defiant manner continues:

HERMIONE (continued)

The bug which you would fright me with I seek.
She pauses to see how this affects Leontes. He

is stony. She speaks to him as though he is a fool not understanding what he has done to her:

HERMIONE (continued)
To me can life be no commodity.

Now she softens somewhat:

HERMIONE (continued)
The crown and comfort of my life, your favor, I do give lost, for I feel it gone,

Now she allows some genuine confusion to color her manner:

HERMIONE (continued)
But know not how it went.

This color of confusion fades as she begins her indictment of Leontes, listing the rest of the wrongs done to her. Her tone is colored with righteous anger:

HERMIONE (continued)
My second joy
And first-fruits of my body, from his presence I am barred as one infectious. My third comfort, Starred most unluckily,

Here he slows down putting extra emphasis on each word. She is accusing him:

HERMIONE (continued)
is from my breast,
The innocent milk in it most innocent mouth, Haled out to murder.

She pauses a moment to let this murder of what she knows to be their child land on him. She switches now to the outrage of being publicly humiliated and denied her rights as a new mother. The underlying feeling here is, "How dare you?":

HERMIONE (continued)
Myself on every post
Proclaimed a strumpet, with immodest hatred
The childbed privilege denied which 'longs
To women of all fashion;

She finishes her indictment which sums up why she finds no advantage to living:

HERMIONE (continued)
 Lastly, hurried
Here to this place 'i the open air before
I have got strength of limit. Now, my liege,
Tell me what blessings I have here alive,
That I should fear to die? Therefore proceed.

She fights not for life, but for her honor, her reputation:

HERMIONE (continued)
But yet, hear this, mistake me not, no life-
I prize it not a straw-but for mine honor,
Which I would free, if I shall be condemned
Upon surmises, all proofs sleeping else
But what your jealousies awake, I tell you
T'is rigor and not law. Your Honors all,
I do refer me to the oracle.
Apollo be my judge.

If we were unjustly accused of infidelity by our spouse, we would certainly feel many emotions coursing through us. Emotions careening from disbelief to shock to righteous anger to deepest hurt and all shades of these in between would course through us from one moment to the next.

As a result of this false charge, Leontes forbids contact between Hermione and their young son, takes her newborn daughter away from her and threatens to have the child killed, has her dragged to a mock trial before giving her a chance to recover from childbirth, proclaims that her life hangs in the balance and proclaims her a whore.

If we go by our feeling life we can easily find ourselves in the angry and defiant emotions expressed in this version of the monologue and reflect them back onto Hermione. The question is, are these reactions of ours true to her?

Often actors stop with this initial "hit" on the character because it feels so right and they never explore any further. And it *does* feel good to be able to line up emotionally with a character right away. It is even a valuable step in the process. But keeping a healthy skepticism alive will often uncover aspects of the character we missed by locking ourselves down too early.

Examining the words, thought patterns and behaviors are the way to test whether or not our initial feelings, thoughts and behaviors match up with *hers*.

It is important to stress here that there is not only one single way to perform any scene, monologue or character. There are however, choices that can serve the play and the character better than others.

What can we discern from the play about the way Hermione thinks, feels and behaves? This is crucial to aligning ourselves with her and will result in a performance of the monologue that is both true to ourselves *and* to her.

Earlier in the play, Act II, Sc. i, is when Leontes first accuses

Hermione of the infidelity and betrayal he is so certain occurred between his wife and Polixenes and banishes her to prison.

Hermione is utterly blindsided by these charges. We need to know how she reacts to these thoroughly unfounded charges and to her imprisonment. What words does she use and how do they differ from the ones we might use in such a situation? How is she thinking and how does that differ from the way that we are thinking? Exploring these questions will be useful to finding ourselves in her and likely change our approach to the monologue from Act III, Sc. ii.

Below is part of that earlier scene from Act II, Sc. i:

LEONTES

...I have said
She's an adulteress, I have said with whom.
More, she's a traitor, and Camillo is
A federary with her; and one that knows,
What she should shame to know herself
But with her most vile principle, that she's
A bedswerver, even as bad as those
That vulgars give bold'st titles-aye and privy
To this their late escape.

HERMIONE

No, by my life,
Privy to none of this. How will this grieve you
When you shall come to clearer knowledge, that
You thus have published me! Gentle my lord,
You scarce can right me thoroughly then to say
You did mistake.

LEONTES

No. If I mistake

125

In those foundations which I build upon,
The center is not big enough to bear
A schoolboy's top. Away with her, to prison!
He who shall speak for her is afar-off guilty
But that he speaks.

HERMIONE

There's some ill planet reigns.
I must be patient till the Heavens look
With an aspect more favorable. Good my lords,
I am not prone to weeping, as our sex
Commonly are, the want of which vain dew
Perchance will dry your pities. But I have
That honorable grief lodged here which burns
Worse than tears drown. Beseech you all, my lords,
With thoughts so qualified as your charities
Shall best instruct you, measure me. And so
The King's will be performed!

LEONTES

Shall I be heard?

HERMIONE

Who is't that goes with me? For you see
My plight requires it. Do not weep good fools,
There is no cause. When you shall know your mistress
Has deserved prison, then abound in tears
As I come out. This action I go on
Is for my better grace. Adieu, my lord.
I never wished to see you sorry, now
I trust I shall. My women, come, you have leave.

LEONTES

Go, do our bidding. Hence!

(Exit Queen, guarded with Ladies.)

Again, some of these words and phrases need explanation. When Leontes says that Camillo is a "federary with her," he means that Camillo and Hermione were confederates of Polixenes aiding him in his escape with Camillo from Sicilia. When Leontes says that:

> "...she's a bedswerver, even as bad as those
> That vulgars give bold'st titles-

he is saying that Hermione hops from bed to bed and is no different from those women for which the lower classes have special terms or "titles."

Then he has a new thought, saying:

> -aye and privy
> To this their late escape."

Here he means again that Hermione was in on the escape of Polixenes and Camillo which, again, she was not.

These lines also need clarification:

> ....If I mistake
> In those foundations which I build upon,
> The center is not big enough to bear
> A schoolboy's top.

Here, Leontes means this: If the strong case I have made against Hermione is wrong, then the center of the Earth is not strong enough to hold a schoolboy's hat.

When he says, "He who shall speak for her is afar-off guilty but that he speaks," he is saying that the simple act of speaking up for his wife makes a person guilty.

How does Hermione react to all of this, what are her thoughts? After Leontes' blistering attack on her how does she respond?

Remarkably, Hermione does not think of herself first, but of her husband. She grieves for the great pain he will feel when he realizes the terrible error of his actions and discovers the truth of her innocence.

When he tells her that he has made no mistake she once again refuses to attack back. Instead, she assigns his irrational behavior to a malevolent planet in the heavens; some misalignment must be the cause of his distemper.

She may well be stunned and shocked at Leontes's behavior, but there is no reactive passion in her words. She explains to the lords in attendance at this arraignment that she is not one given easily to tears as one might expect of a woman in this situation. Neither does it seem that she is given to vitriol or vindictiveness. While both tears and righteous anger would certainly be understandable from anyone in her circumstance, that does not seem to be her way.

No, it is the burning grief she feels for her besmirched honor that scalds her. She asks the lords who know her to measure her character and to see if they find any grain of truth in the accusations leveled against her. In the next moment, she proclaims that the King's will to have her imprisoned be carried out. She offers no resistance to it.

What thought patterns are going on inside of Hermione's mind that would justify her behavior here? Why does she accept Leontes's imprisonment of her without heavy resistance?

Where do we find this same extraordinary sense of grace that Hermione seems to possess in ourselves? Where is it? How do we ensoul her?

For that is the issue here. If we are truthful with ourselves, then we would acknowledge the fact that we would not likely behave so admirably as does Hermione. We would ultimately lose patience with the injustice of these accusations and fight back with every tool we had.

So, has Shakespeare drawn a character that cannot be really be played, a character that is a saint? If Hermione's thought patterns and behaviors are consistently like this throughout the play, then we face the daunting task of making a saint, a human.

Your or my reaction at suddenly being accused of an infidelity we did not even conceive of committing and being sent to prison for an act that never happened would likely be different from Hermione's. She, although she must be stunned and in shock, blames not her husband but some nefarious intent of a planet. She is able, somehow, to remain calm and is patient enough to wait until the Heavens are in a more benevolent nood for this unjust punishment to be reversed. This is not a person who panics easily.

This is what is apparently different in her from us. So again we ask, how is Hermione thinking about what is happening to her and how do we merge ourselves with that thinking? First we need to know how she is processing Leontes's sudden shift in behavior.

Looking at her words we see that she is perceiving him as in the grips of some sort of sickness; that he is being driven by some external influence ("ill planet") and is therefore not himself. So, if it is truly *not* Leontes acting this way, then he is not responsible for his words or actions. No, she reasons, some unseen force is directing his jealousy and when it spends itself, his sanity will return.

Now, if she is thinking this way it adds a second meaning to the "grief" she feels. It is not only grief for her honor, but grief for his condition. From her point of view, *he* is the one suffering most here, not her.

Where is this way of thinking in us? How can we merge our thought with hers and find the emotions that are authentically stimulated by this perception of him?

Rather than use a personal experience, which would certainly be a valid and useful approach, let us use an experience we could easily imagine. If our dearly loved partner suddenly became irrationally jealous of the way we talked to his or her best friend, suggesting that we were having an affair with them and flying into a rage about it in public, we would most likely try calm our partner down and absolutely dissuade them of this false notion. This is precisely what Hermione does in a passage just prior to the one quoted above.

Now, if our jealous partner disbelieved every denial we made and continued making all kinds of cruel accusations and threats, we would be shocked, embarrassed, frightened, hurt, confused and worried and if we had never before seen such behavior in our partner, we would not know what was going on or what to do about it, but we would be deeply alarmed.

We would also feel sorry to see them suffering over a baseless fiction, lost in the grips of a delusional fantasy. We would grieve for ourselves that our partner could ever suspect us of such behavior and grieve to see them torturing themselves for no reason. And while we would not ascribe the cause of such behavior to the stars or the planets, we would wonder about some psychological disturbance inside of them that would need the attention of a therapist, psychologist or psychiatrist.

This we can understand and finding the truth of this way of thinking in ourselves aligns our thoughts with hers and when this occurs it is almost automatic for our feeling lives and behaviors to match up with hers as well. We are finding ourselves in her and realizing that how Hermione reacts to Leontes's misguided jealousy is only apparently different from ours and that we can erase that difference by shifting our outrage and anger to concern and empathy for our loved one who is like a person in the grip of a narcotic, no longer in control of himself.

As Leontes consigns Hermione to prison her ladies in waiting, not believing what they are witnessing, weep for her. But Hermione both berates and comforts them. She instructs them to stop their weeping because there is no reason for them to cry, since she has done nothing wrong. If they are going to weep, she tells them, do it when she is actually guilty of some misdeed, but not until that time.

Remarkably, she is comforting her attendants at this moment and not bemoaning her state. Is this the unrealistically "ideal" behavior of a fairy tale? Possibly, but if you know that not a shred of evidence exists to corroborate the charges made against you, it is not hard to imagine the consolation this provides you knowing that in the end, the truth will prevail and you will be vindicated.

If you are accused of infidelity and you have nothing to hide, there is relief in that. If you are guilty however, the anxiety of being found out would be next to impossible to manage. The truth of this is obvious both in the fiction Shakespeare has created and in the truth of real life.

Now, our thought that Hermione's grief is as much for Leontes's error as for her own honor is confirmed when Hermione says goodbye to Leontes on her way to prison:

> HERMIONE
> I never wished to see you sorry, now
> I trust I shall.

This could be said bitterly, ironically, vindictively or in any number of ways. But to me, it seems to align best with Hermione's thoughts and emotions if enunciated with a regretful sympathy conveying the thought that she will take no joy in what is sure to be his future suffering.

What is emerging to us about this character, Hermione? Is she only acting the way she is in order to protect herself from her husband's rage? Is she just telling him what he wants to hear, or is she honest with him?

We know from a later scene, just after the monologue we will revisit from Act III, Sc. ii, that the oracle from Delphi declares to all present, including Leontes, that she is innocent and not an adulteress and that Leontes is wrong in all of his suspicions, including the supposed betrayal with Camillo. From this we know that in her earlier scenes she has spoken nothing but the truth to her husband, that she is not dissembling in any way.

We know that the love Hermione bears for her son Mamillius is so profoundly deep that when he dies from worry over his mother's plight, she faints and quickly passes away from the shock and grief of his passing.

Does this really happen? Do people die from shock and grief? Maybe. But in this case there is more to the story as we will see from the monologue.

Does she blame Leontes for the mad jealous actions that lead both to their son's death and to her own? No.

When she comes back to life in Act V, Sc. iii (yes, she comes back to life), her first act is to embrace her husband. Blame is not her way, forgiveness is.

Her first and only words in the scene are to Perdita, the daughter that Leontes ordered killed, but who has survived:

HERMIONE
You gods, look down,
And from your sacred vials pour your graces
Upon my daughter's head! Tell me, mine own,
Where hast thou been preserved? Where lived?
     How found
Thy father's Court? For thou shalt hear that I,
Knowing by Paulina that the oracle
Gave hope thou wast in being, have preserved
Myself to see the issue.

Hermione is telling Perdita here that it was the hope that her daughter was alive that allowed Hermione to preserve herself from death so that she might see Perdita again.

So, Hermione dies for love of her son and lives again for love of her daughter. Knowing what we now know of Hermione through her words, her thoughts and her actions we can begin to assemble an approach to her monologue in Act III in a more informed way.

Our initial approach came from our own truthful anger and outrage at Leontes for the cruel and inhuman punishments he metes out to his wife. Now, although the cruel and inhuman punishments remain the same, we see her thoughts, emotions and behaviors differently.

Hermione is a loving person. She feeds on the praise of her husband, loves her son, is innocent of even a hint of indiscretion, tells only the truth, forgives her husband and somehow stays alive after death just so she can see the daughter she gave birth to. She is patient even in the face of great wrongs, and values her honor more than her life.

This is the portrait of an admirable character. The facets of ourselves that feel vindictiveness, rage, cruelty and self-righteousness are of little use in playing her now. We realize that through Hermione we are afforded the rare privilege of reflecting truthfully back the best of ourselves.

Here is the monologue as it might be performed with the view of Hermione we now working with. Hermione is summoned from prison by Leontes having just recently given birth to their daughter, Perdita. Below is the full indictment read by an officer to her and those in attendance:

OFFICER
(Reads.) "Hermione, Queen to the worthy Leontes, King of Sicilia, thou art here accused and arraigned of high treason, in committing adul-

tery with Polixenes, King of Bohemia, and conspiring with Camillo to take away the life of our Sovereign, Lord the King, thy royal husband. The pretense whereof being by circumstances partly laid open, thou, Hermione, contrary to the faith and allegiance of a true subject, didst counsel and aid them, for their better safety, to fly away by night."

Hermione responds to these charges by saying that Leontes knows her to be constant and true and that she did not help Polixenes and Camillo to escape from Sicilia. He is deaf to her words and threatens her with death:

LEONTES
….You had a bastard by Polixenes…so thou
Shalt feel our justice, in whose easiest passage
Look for no more than death.

Hermione is unsteady on her feet. She has been imprisoned and probably been only meagerly fed. She has likely been treated as a traitorous criminal and accorded none of the courtesies of her station. She has also very recently given birth and has not yet had the proper time to recover from that ordeal as she clearly states in her monologue below. This weakened condition contributes powerfully to her collapse and death when she learns that her son has died.

Hermione speaks as if out of breath and with no fear, only with a kind of exhausted and weary voice. She is calm:

HERMIONE
Sir, spare your threats.

She pauses a moment to take a breath:

HERMIONE (continued)
The bug which you would frighten me with I
seek.

*There is a rueful smile on her face as she again
pauses to make sure this statement lands on
Leontes. He looks at her, puzzled. She should
be frightened of his threatened sentence, but is
not. She explains:*

HERMIONE (continued)
To me can life be no commodity.

*She continues now with regret, puzzlement and
pain, as she begins to explain to him why it is
that life no longer presents any advantages to
her:*

HERMIONE (continued)
The crown and comfort of my life, your favor,
I do give lost, for I do feel it gone,

*There is a pause here as tears well up behind
her eyes:*

HERMIONE (continued)
But know not how it went.

*She seems lost for a moment, then gathers her-
self and speaks in disbelief. It is as if she has no
understanding how this could be:*

HERMIONE (continued)
My second joy
And first-fruits of my body, from his presence
I am barred as one infectious.

135

She places both hands on her stomach:

HERMIONE (continued)
My third comfort,
Starred most unluckily, is from my breast,
The innocent milk in it most innocent mouth,
Haled out to murder. Myself on every post
Proclaimed a strumpet, with immodest hatred
The childbed privilege denied which 'longs
To women of all fashion;

She kneels onto one knee, not to beg, but to conserve her strength.

HERMIONE (continued)
lastly, hurried
Here to this place I' the open air before
I have got strength of limit.

She looks up at Leontes, concluding her argument that life has no hold on her:

Now my liege,
Tell me what blessings I have here alive,
That I should fear to die? Therefore proceed.

It seems that she is finished, but now rises to stand on both feet:

HERMIONE (continued)
But yet hear this,

Leontes nods his head knowingly as if he knows she is now, as he expected, going to plead for mercy. Hermione sees his look:

HERMIONE (continued)
mistake me not, no life-

She looks out at the lords in attendance who are murmuring:

HERMIONE (continued)
I prize it not a straw-

She does not continue until the lords are silent. She looks back at Leontes. Hermione's voice begins to rise with a steely quality in it as she judges her judge:

HERMIONE (continued)
but for mine honor,
Which I would free, if I shall be condemned
Upon surmises, all proofs sleeping else
But what your jealousies awake, I tell you
'Tis rigor and not law.

She looks to the lords and back at Leontes and speaks with a sure voice, having regained some of her strength:

HERMIONE (continued)
Your honors all,
I do refer me to the oracle.
Apollo be my judge!

It is important to reiterate there that there is no single, definitive way to play this scene or any other. But if we can make others feel, during the course of the evening, that it could go not possibly go any other way, then we will have done a worthy thing.

The test for determining the usefulness of any approaches is this: Does the choice correspond to evidence in the text and illuminate it, or does the choice confuse and obscure it? Final choices should, of course, be determined in a collaboration between the actor and the director.

I stated earlier that Hermione has no use for our rage and self-righteousness, but the actor in the example above put real steel in her voice and manner for the last lines and it did not seem at all to violate the character. It worked so well because it was a matter of degree. It read not so much as rage, but as resolve, as conviction. So I was wrong and very happy that the actor was not afraid to put some level of outrage and anger in her manner. *Her instincts were better than my analysis.*

Could Hermione be calm, without that new strength in her voice when she says "Your honors all, I do refer me to the oracle. Apollo be my judge?" Yes, that would be perfectly fine so long as the actor is truthfully connected herself to this choice.

Could she be consumed with silly laughter when she says this line? It would be hard to justify, unless she was drunk or high on drugs and how would such a choice align with the character?

If you find yourself going through tortuous explanations as to why a certain choice would be a good one, it is usually a sign that you are trying to force it onto the character, trying to fit a round peg into a square hole. And while such a choice might be interesting and entertaining in the moment, and would certainly be unconventional, how would it serve the larger conception of the character and the play? "Interesting" choices sometime sacrifice the long arc of the character for a local effect. Keep on the lookout for this.

But also keep in mind that there are many other ways to play this scene that would not violate the character, but rather illuminate it.

So, by changing the character thought, we made significant adjustments to our original approach to the monologue. At first, we personalized our reaction to Leontes's unjust accusations, thinking him cruel and sadistic.

Then, as we examined the circumstances of the play, the words Hermione uses and the thoughts that powered those words, we were led to thinking of him as unable to free himself from behaviors and feelings that he could not control. This resulted in behaviors and feelings from us that were quite different from our initial ones.

This new perception of him enabled us to shift our reactions and thoughts closer to hers. In our own experience we understand finding patience with someone who cannot let go of a fixation because they are not really themselves and therefore, are not to blame.

Instead, we want to get through to them, strive to help them shake off their psychic disturbance. We do not attack them. When we think in *this* way, we are thinking like Hermione. And when we find that place where her thoughts and ours can merge, we can then begin to ensoul her, find ourselves genuinely feeling, reacting and behaving in the ways that she does, because we discover that *we are no different from her.* What Hermione sees before her is now what we see before us; a good man whom we deeply love in the grips of a frightful mania.

Now, if we only demonstrate our understanding of her situation without actually feeling it and believing it, then we are standing back behind her, not with her, disengaged and ineffective. If however, we *experience* these thoughts and emotions *with* her, then we have achieved our goal of personalizing in character.

CHAPTER SIX

SHYLOCK, *THE MERCHANT OF VENICE*

Shylock the money lender is the most famous character from Shakespeare's play, *The Merchant of Venice.* Over the centuries many interpretations of him have been presented.

In the early years he was portrayed as a comedic figure to be scorned and laughed at. This version of him then evolved into a vile, greedy and evil character whose need for blood revenge overrides any sense of mercy or decency in him. A figure to be despised.

After the Holocaust of World War II it became impossible to present the character in either of these ways. The undeniable anti-Semitism of the play had to be upended, inoculated against. In order to accomplish this, Shylock had to be seen in a more sympathetic light, as a victim of religious and cultural prejudice.

Shakespeare creates in Shylock a truly dimensional character with both good and bad traits. Some of the speeches that Shakespeare provides for him are powerfully eloquent and elicit a deep sympathy for him. On the other hand, his actions in the play are detestable and evoke disgust and revulsion from us.

The challenge in playing him lies in balancing these opposing aspects of his nature. Some performers emphasize the sympathetic parts of him while ignoring the darker aspects of his character while others highlight the vengeful side of him, devaluing his deep sensitivities.

Those that seek to minimize the more vicious facets of Shylock's character usually present him as a calm and dignified figure, shortchanging his righteous and angry outbursts. Those who wish to foreground his wrathful and righteous fury often miss the cool and calculating aspects of his character. Neither of these approaches is fully satisfactory because they flatten out his complexity.

The truth is that Shylock is both a victim and a victimizer. He is empathetic to us because of the debasements he endures at the hands of prejudiced Christians. But, he is also repellent to us because of his savage blood lust.

Ensouling him means allowing all aspects of his character to light up the facets in us and then truthfully reflecting them back. His righteous anger is not difficult to find in ourselves, especially for those who have ever been bullied. The scheming, manipulative and murderous side of him is perhaps less easily contacted. Although we have certainly felt such feelings, they usually dissipate over time. On the other hand, some grudges can last a lifetime.

But there is more to him than just these two facets. Shylock is also a deep feeling and loving man. This may seem a surprising statement, but as we learn more about him we will discover the truth of it and find a deep way to ensoul his dimensionality.

When we first meet Shylock he is in an unusual situation. He is being asked by Bassanio to grant a loan to Shylock's great enemy, Antonio. Bassanio needs money in order to woo the woman with whom he is in love. He has asked his friend Antonio for the money, but Antonio cannot help him because all of his fortune is in cargo ships currently at sea.

Antonio asks Bassanio to search Venice to see if Antonio's credit is good enough for someone to loan him the money so he can, in turn, loan it back to Bassanio. In the end, Bassanio comes to Shylock with the loan proposal and Shylock considers it:

ACT I, Sc. iii
[Enter Bassanio and Shylock]

SHYLOCK
Three thousand ducats. Well.

BASSANIO
Aye, sir, for three months.

SHYLOCK
For three months. Well.

BASSANIO
For the which, as I told you, Antonio shall be bound.

SHYLOCK
Antonio shall become bound. Well.

BASSANIO
May you stead me? Will you pleasure me? Shall I know your answer?

SHYLOCK
Three thousand ducats for three months, and Antonio bound.

BASSANIO
Your answer to that.

SHYLOCK
Antonio is a good man.

BASSANIO
Have you heard any imputation to the contrary?

SHYLOCK
Oh, no, no, no, no. My meaning in saying that

> he is a good man is to have you understand me that he is sufficient. Yet his means are in supposition. He hath as argosy bound to Tripolis, another to the Indies. I understand, moreover, upon the Rialto, he hath a third at Mexico, a fourth for England, and other ventures he hath, squandered Abroad. But ships are but boards, sailors but men. There be land rats and water rats, water thieves and land thieves-I mean pirates. And then there is the peril of waters, winds, and rocks. The man is, notwithstanding, sufficient. Three thousand ducats. I think I may take his bond.

The scene continues with a couple of exchanges before Antonio enters, but there is much here to parse.

But first, as always, we need to be certain of the meaning of every word and phrase. A "ducat" at the time was worth about two dollars. So the loan amount would be approximately six thousand dollars.

Bassanio asks, "Will you stead me?" This means will you "help" me. When Shylock says that Antonio is "sufficient," he means that Antonio is solvent and therefore should be able to repay the loan.

Bassanio has obviously presented the loan proposal to Shylock just before the beginning of the scene, so we are picking them up in mid-conversation. Shylock is confirming the loan amount, the terms of it and who it is that will be in debt to him if he grants it. He says the simple word, "Well" each time after he receives assurance that he has the terms correctly understood.

There is much in this "Well." It hints at some interior thought and implies some behavior as well. If we take his "Well" to mean "I see," it suggests that he is mulling over whether or not to accept or to deny Bassanio's request.

When Shylock does not immediately answer the impatient Bassanio when he asks, "May you stead me? Will you pleasure me? Your answer?" it implies that he is continuing to take time in considering the proposal, thinking it all through with great deliberation. Even after Bassanio's three questions, Shylock still does not answer him, but instead reiterates the conditions of the loan. It is hard not to imagine that Shylock is teasing out this negotiation in order to increase Bassanio's anxiety.

This proposition is a dream come true for Shylock. Antonio is a rich merchant who has often made loans to others with no interest in order to thwart Shylock's money lending business and Shylock hates him for this. Beyond that, Antonio has verbally abused him and the Hebrew religion, spit on him and kicked him. Suddenly the opportunity to pay Antonio back for his abuses over the years is right in front of him. He would love to have Antonio in his debt, but he cannot afford to seem that way to Bassanio, so he plays hard to get.

He enumerates to Bassanio the reasons why such a loan to Antonio would be risky: His fortune is on cargo ships bound for different ports and ships are vulnerable to dangerous weather conditions, to sailor error and to thieving pirates. These reasons are all valid ones and they must redouble Bassanio's apprehension.

But in the end, Shylock agrees to grant the loan. Why? What is Shylock thinking that allows him to take on this risky financial venture?

During this short exchange with Bassanio and possibly even before, when Bassanio first proposes the loan to him offstage, Shylock has been formulating a plan. He knows that Antonio despises him because he feels that Shylock charges exorbitant interest rates on the loans he makes, as all Jews do.

Imagine what a surprise it would be to Antonio if Shylock charged him no interest at all on this loan. That would utterly confound him. And what if such an offer was presented to him as a gesture of friendship? Would Antonio actually be grateful to him?

And what if he could tie a seemingly whimsical penalty to the loan terms if Antonio defaulted? Something like taking a pound of his flesh? Could he get him to agree to that? It seems worth a try.

Now, this devious strategy could only come to pass if Antonio's ships actually do meet with grievous misfortune on the high seas and the odds of that occurring are very low. But if it did happen, then Shylock would finally be able take the blood revenge on his enemy that he lusts for.

This is a lot of scheming to do in a short period of time, but it seems that during his brief interaction with Bassanio that this is precisely how Shylock is thinking.

This level of craftiness must have been brewing for many years, and Shylock cannot allow Bassanio to detect it, so he takes his time looking like he is considering the proposition when in fact, he is also considering how to use this opportunity to gain an advantage over Antonio.

Immediately after agreeing to the loan, Shylock asks to speak directly to Antonio who soon enters. When he does, Shylock has this to say about him in a soliloquy:

SHYLOCK
(Aside) How like a fawning publican he looks!
I hate him for he is a Christian,
But more for that in low simplicity
He lends out money gratis and brings down
The rate of usance here with us in Venice.
If I can catch him once upon the hip,
I will feed fat the ancient grudge I bear him.
He hates our sacred nation, and he rails,

Even there where merchants most do congregate,
On me, my bargains, and my well-worn thrift,
Which he calls interest. Cursed be my tribe
If I forgive him.

A "publican" was a Roman tax collector and a figure to be detested.

On first glance it looks as though Shylock hates Antonio because he is a Christian, but that is not the source of his greatest antipathy towards him. Instead, it is the fact that Antonio gives out loans and charges no interest on them that arouses Shylock's greater hostility.

What does Shylock mean by catching Antonio "upon the hip?" This is a term borrowed from the wrestling arena where if one can catch the opponent on the hip, then he can be throw him to the ground. So, if the plan he has just devised can be put into action, then Shylock can throw Antonio to the ground and avenge not only his own personal grievances, but those of the Jewish People as well.

Shylock soon tries to explain to Antonio, through the use of a biblical story, that he is going to grant him an interest free loan. But Antonio is suspicious of him and turns to Bassanio saying, "The Devil can quote scripture for his purpose," meaning that Shylock is using the Bible to justify his taking of interest. He then asks Shylock if he is going to loan him the requested sum:

ANTONIO
Well, Shylock, shall we be beholding to you?

This question triggers the following monologue:

SHYLOCK
Signior Antonio, many a time and oft

In the Rialto you have rated me
About my monies and my usances.
Still have I borne it with a patient shrug,
For sufferance is the badge of all out tribe.
You call me disbeliever, cutthroat dog,
And spit upon my Jewish gabardine,
And all for use of that which is mine own.
Well then it now appears you need my help.
Go to, then, you come to me and you say,
"Shylock we would have monies." You say so,
You that did void your rheum upon my beard
And foot me as you spurn a stranger cur
Over your threshold. Money is your suit.
What should I say to you? Should I not say,
"Hath a dog money? Is it possible
A cur can lend three thousand ducats?" Or
Shall I bend low and in a bondsman's key,
With bated breath and whispering humbleness,
Say this-
"Fair sir, you spit on me Wednesday last,
You spurned me such a day, another time
You called me dog, and for these courtesies
I'll lend you thus much monies?"

Before we consider different ways to play this monologue we must understand what Shylock is saying on a literal level.

The "Rialto" refers to a commercial center in Venice,
Italy where a great deal of business is conducted. The word
"rated" is shortened from "berated." "Usances" refers to the
interest charged on borrowed funds. The word "sufferance"
here means "patience."

So, in the Rialto Antonio has many times berated Shylock for the high level of interest he charges on the loans he

makes and shylock has born it patiently because that is what all Jews have to do.

Beyond this verbal abuse that Shylock says he has shrugged off as simply the expected treatment of Jews by Christians, Antonio has also spit on his Jewish "gabardine." This word refers to Shylock's tunic. "Go to, then" means, "All right, then." A few lines later Shylock notes that Antonio has also spit on his beard; the word "rheum" refers here to spit.

In addition to these grievances, Antonio has not only called Shylock a "dog," he has also kicked him as if he was some stray dog trying to enter Antonio's house: "And foot me as you spurn a stranger cur over your threshold."

So, Antonio has publicly shamed Shylock for his greedy loan rates, insulted him, spit on his face and his clothes and kicked him. How has Shylock reacted? He has endured it all, he says, with patience. Now, this man wants financial help from him. Quite the unexpected turn of events.

How does Shylock react? He mocks Antonio by asking him if a dog can lend money, or if he should kneel down like a slave ("bondman") and thank him for all of the abuses he has suffered, which he ironically refers to as "courtesies."

The words of Shakespeare are so delicious here, penned with such vivid imagery and sarcastic contempt that we cannot resist them. The opportunity to exact some just retribution for such egregious mistreatment is something we understand and can easily identify with.

Now let us return to the monologue in question. The following is one way to approach it using our thoughts and feelings with regard to Shylock's hatred of Antonio which we can easily locate in ourselves. Those who bully us, spit on us and kick us deserve no less:

ANTONIO
Well, Shylock, shall we be beholding to you?

Looks Antonio directly in the eyes, and speaks with barely contained rage:

SHYLOCK
Signior Antonio, many a time and oft
In the Rialto you have rated me
About my moneys and my usances.

Shylock looks away trying to find a level of calm:

SHYLOCK (continued)
Still have I born it with a patient shrug,
For sufferance is the badge of all our tribe.

The anger rises again and rises on the word "spit":

SHYLOCK (continued)
You call me disbeliever, cutthroat dog,
And spit upon my Jewish gabardine,

With an increased level of outrage:

SHYLOCK (continued)
And all for use of that which is mine own.

Taking a moment to settle down:

SHYLOCK (continued)
Well, then, it now appears you need my help.

Shylock takes a moment here, knowing that Antonio is waiting to see if he will be helped or not. Then he unleashes on Antonio:

SHYLOCK (continued)
Go to, then, you come to me and you say
"Shylock we would have moneys." You say so,

Now with real vehemence and pointing at Antonio on the word, "You":

SHYLOCK (continued)
You that did void your rheum upon my beard
And foot me as you spurn a stranger cur
Over your threshold.

Speaking now with disdain:

SHYLOCK (continued)
Moneys is your suit.

Now in a deliberate and quiet voice:

SHYLOCK (continued)
What should I say to you?

He waits for an answer from Antonio, putting him on the spot. No answer is forthcoming. Shylocks voice drips with sarcasm:

SHYLOCK (continued)
Should I not say,
"Hath a dog money?

He waits again for an answer that he knows will not come.

SHYLOCK (continued)
Is it possible
A dog can lend three thousand ducats?" Or

Shall I bend low and in a bondman's key,
With bated breath and whispering humbleness
Say this-

He bends down in mock supplication:

SHYLOCK (continued)
"Fair sir, you spit upon me on Wednesday last,
You spurned me such a day, another time
You called me dog, and for these courtesies,

*Shylock straightens up, and speaks slowly with
great disdain in his voice:*

SHYLOCK (continued)
I'll lend you thus much moneys?"

Anger, contempt and mockery are here in large measure. And these emotions feel appropriate and satisfying because of how empowering it is to strike back at the person who has abused you.

This monologue can validly be performed in this way and I have seen it done several times like this, with minor variations, and it is always deeply connected to the actor.

But there is a problem. The problematic issue crops up immediately with the next two exchanges between Antonio and Shylock as Antonio reacts to Shylock's indictment of him with defiant anger:

ANTONIO
I am as like to call thee so again,
To spit on thee again, to spurn thee too.
If thou wilt lend this money, lend it not
As to thy friends, for when did friendship take
A breed for barren metal of his friend?

But lend it rather to thine enemy,
Who if he break, thou mayst with better face
Exact the penalty.

SHYLOCK
Why look you how you storm!
I would be friends with you, and have your love,
Forget the shames that you have stained me with,
Supply your present wants, and take no doit
Of usance for my moneys, and you'll not hear me.
This is kind I offer.

Shylock is surprised at the vehemence of Antonio's words and cannot understand what has triggered them. If Shylock has himself been "storming," then such a response would be expected. But it seems from this exchange that Shylock has not been storming at Antonio during his monologue. Instead, he has been behaving in some other way.

In the monologue it seems that Shylock is not trying to inflame Antonio at all. Yes, the words are harsh, but perhaps they are not harshly said. It may well be the case in this monologue that Shylock is not trying to attack Antonio at all, but has a much different purpose in mind. What could that be?

Shylock does not simply want to vent at Antonio. What Shylock wants in this scene is to *make a deal*. If he is screaming at and cutting Antonio to the quick in the monologue before the deal is made, he jeopardizes the chances that Antonio will agree to the loan terms.

It is certainly true that our first reaction to the monologue was legitimately based on the circumstances of the play and that it felt like we had a deep personal grasp of Shylock's thinking and of his outrage. But the text is telling us a different story.

This may be one of those situations where an actor gives in to the strong lure of a local moment and winds up damaging a longer range thought or goal. In other words, the local moment here is giving payback to Antonio with a satisfying emotional blast, while the longer range thought is getting him on our side so we can make the deal we want. After all, we do not want to alienate someone with whom we are hoping to make a deal. Getting him to agree to the default penalty is of far greater importance to Shylock than is scalding Antonio with his rage. Shylock is playing a long game here, not a short one.

If we are right about this, then we need to alter our approach to the monologue so that we can more accurately locate *Shylock's* thinking and behavior.

Before we proceed, it may be properly pointed out to us that we are wrong in our analysis and that Shylock is indeed, thinking about charging interest because just before the monologue there is this brief exchange:

SHYLOCK
Three thousand ducats. 'Tis a good round sum.
Three months from twelve-then, let me see, the rate-

ANTONIO
Well, Shylock, shall we be beholding to you?

As we know, Shylock's monologue is his answer to Antonio's question. So yes, it does appear that Shylock *is* calculating the interest rate he will impose and Antonio naturally wants to know how much in debt to Shylock he will be.

How do we reconcile this with the thought that Shylock does *not* intend to charge Antonio any interest on the loan? The answer to this question will help to clarify an alternative approach to the monologue.

154

Before he is cut off by Antonio's question, this is the surprise that Shylock is about to spring: He is about to say that the rate will be nothing, zero. This is what he is thinking, what he intends to say and this is why Shylock is so surprised when Antonio storms at him.

In other words, Shylock is telling Antonio that has him all wrong, that he wants to be a friend to him, not an enemy. That if he hadn't been interrupted just before the monologue that he was going to say tell Antonio that he was not going to charge him even a penny of interest on the loan. Shylock's full thought is this: "Three months from twelve-then, let me see, the rate-*will be zero.*" But before he can announce this to him, Antonio bitterly asks his question.

Remember to keep in mind that before his ensuing monologue Shylock has explained, through the use of a biblical story that he will not be charging any interest to Antonio, but does not yet realize that Antonio has misconstrued his meaning. He does know however, that Antonio seems to have characterized his story as trickery.

So, what then is Shylock's thinking as he begins the monologue? It is this: "You know you have been quite abusive to me over the years and I have every reason to charge you an exorbitant interest rate, and you have every reason to expect that I will. If you were in my position, you would do the same, wouldn't you? But, I am not going to do this at all, as I have already explained."

If someone came to you asking for a favor who has been a personal enemy to you, disrespecting both your beliefs and your entire way of life to the point where they have kicked you and spat on you, you would not be inclined to lift a finger to help them.

However, if you needed something from them (say, a signature on a legal document), then you might want, at least temporarily, to conceal your animosity in the cloak of friendship. This may be devious, but deviousness is not above any of us in the right circumstance.

In the monologue, Shylock is certainly reminding Antonio of the great wrongs that Antonio has done to him. But by doing so and then forgiving him, Shylock can then appear as a man of great magnanimity and keep his darker motives hidden. Shylock needs Antonio's trust so that he will agree to the pound of flesh clause that he is about to propose to him. Antonio needs to agree with Shylock that this absurd penalty is nothing but "a merry sport," just as Shylock says it is. This degree of trust cannot be earned by railing at Antonio in the monologue.

If this is how Shylock is thinking, then the feelings and behaviors informing the monologue will necessarily be quite different from our first approach and will, hopefully, cohere better with the rest of the scene.

Below, is *one way* that this shift in thought can manifest in behavior:

As Antonio interrupts him, Shylock notes Antonio's disdainful tone and lowers his head a moment in order to shake off his reactive anger. Then, as he gathers himself, a rueful half-smile crosses his face:

SHYLOCK
Signoir Antonio,

Shylock speaks as if to a naughty schoolboy:

SHYLOCK (continued)
Many a time and oft
In the Rialto you have rated me about my usances.
Shylock shrugs:

SHYLOCK (continued)
Still have I borne it with a patient shrug,
For sufferance is the badge of all our tribe.

Shylock speaks calmly and reasonably, as if reading from a list of the usual epithets so often thrown at him:

SHYLOCK (continued)
You call me misbeliever, cutthroat dog,
And...

He pauses a moment as he swallows back some rising anger because this one hurts:

SHYLOCK (continued)
...spit upon my Jewish gabardine,

He recovers himself and says, quite reasonably, with a small smile on his face:

SHYLOCK (continued)
And all for use of that which is mine own.

He lets this land for a moment on Antonio, then continues :

SHYLOCK (continued)
Well, then, it now appears you need my help.
Go to, then, you come to me and you say
"Shylock, we would have moneys."

He now points a finger at Antonio and allows a tone of anger and accusation into his voice. He isn't much louder, just more pointed:

SHYLOCK (continued)
You say so,
You that did void your rheum upon my beard
And foot me as you spurn a stranger cur
Over your threshold. Moneys is your suit.
What should I say to you? Should I not say,

*A small smile once again comes onto his face
as he delights in needling Antonio with these
unanswerable and sardonic questions. He asks
them simply and waits a moment for an answer
to them that never comes. No raised voice:*

SHYLOCK (continued)
"Hath a dog money? Is it possible
A cur can lend three thousand ducats?" Or

Now, his tone is more biting:

SHYLOCK (continued)
Shall I bend low

He bends at the waist like a servant:

SHYLOCK (continued)
And in a bondman's key,
With bated breath and whispering humbleness,
Say this-

*Adopting the innocent voice of a slave speaking
to his master:*

SHYLOCK (continued)
"Fair sir, you spit upon me on Wednesday last,
You spurned me such a day, another time
You called me dog, and for these courtesies,

With a broad ironic smile on his face, as if to say, "Are you kidding?":

SHYLOCK (continued)
I'll lend you thus much moneys?'"

While there is some anger, resentment and sarcasm evident in Shylock in this version, it is nothing like the scolding and raging we found in the earlier version.

In this version, Shylock is having a bit of fun with Antonio's dependent and awkward position. This is after all, the man who has viciously criticized him for charging exorbitant interest rates and who is now forced to ask him for a loan. What a delicious turn of events this must be for Shylock.

Even though he is taking Antonio to task, Shylock believes he is doing so in a way that will not alienate him. The underlying tone is this: "You've done some pretty awful things to me, but I am not going to berate you for them, just make you feel a little guilty for the way you have treated me." In his mind this tone should not be met with anger or resentment. He is therefore stunned when Antonio reacts with such vitriol and he must scramble to salvage the situation and make clear to Antonio that he wants to be friends with him and will be lending him all the funds he so desperately desires. And Shylock must reiterate one more time again that he will not be charging any interest to Antonio on the loan amount.

Finally, Antonio understands what Shylock is offering, including the bloody penalty that will be imposed in the case of a default, and admits that, "…there is much kindness in the Jew." Shylock has won and leaves to draw up the contract which Antonio will later sign.

We might not think ourselves as calculating as Shylock is in this scene, laying a long range trap for an enemy that might not ever come to pass. But the feeling of paying back someone who has so thoroughly disrespected us both verbally and physically is, frankly, easily aroused.

A psychiatrist once pointed out to me that when someone hurts us we do not want to just hurt them back. Instead, we want to hurt them back ten times more than they hurt us. This is why, he told me, that a person can get into a heated argument in a bar and later return with a gun. In physics he said, there is an equal and opposite reaction, but with people it is not necessarily opposite and definitely not equal. It escalates.

You have felt it and so have I. Someone cuts you off on the freeway, and instantly a wholly disproportionate rage consumes you with stunning speed. Human beings are like this. We hardly ever actually act on these feelings, but they are there. If someone continually bullies or disrespects you, you fantasize about what satisfying revenges you might visit on them. But again, such fantasies are hardly ever acted out in real life. But planning a vengeful act, even in a fantasy, is something we have all done.

In playing Shylock you get the opportunity to explore and experience this side of yourself without actually suffering the consequences.

Up to this point we have a character in Shylock who is manipulative, fierce, full of hatred and vengeful. He certainly has good reasons for these feelings and we can sympathize with him. The question is, can we *empathize* with him? Is there any other aspect of him that will allow us to truly ensoul him? There is.

Shylock has a daughter. Her name is Jessica. He is very strict with her and does not want her mingling with the Christian population, especially the Christian men. Jessica is the only person in the play to whom Shylock confides his misgivings and fears. He is very protective of her and in his own particular way, loves her. But she feels stifled by his diffident and severe manner and says she is "ashamed to be my father's child."

Jessica runs away with Lorenzo, a Christian man with whom she has fallen in love, and leaves Venice with him to a place called Belmont. When Shylock discovers her gone he rouses the Duke of Venice and they go to Bassanio's ship to search for her there. Although it has already sailed they were apparently not on board anyway. Antonio certifies this to the Duke. They were seen instead in a gondola leaving Venice together.

Shylock is heard wandering the streets lamenting about the loss of his daughter and of the money and the jewelry she has stolen from his house. Jessica has even taken the ring given to him by his deceased wife. And when he is told by his friend Tubal that the ring has turned up in Genoa where she used it to purchase a monkey he exclaims:

SHYLOCK

Out upon her! Thou torturest me, Tubal. It was my turquoise, I had it of Leah when I was a bachelor. I would not have given it for a wilderness of monkeys.

This is the only glimpse we have of Shylock's past private life and the first mention of his wife Leah, whom he evidently loved. It is not hard to imagine tears falling from his eyes as he recalls the precious ring and the wife who presented it to him before they married.

He may curse his daughter and wish her dead in this scene, but it is not hard to believe that he says these things about her because she has broken his heart. At this moment, Shylock, blindsided by the betrayal of his daughter, is a broken man. Hard as he is, he is still a human being and this brief window into his aching soul genuinely hurts our hearts.

161

Here is the entry point for deep ensouling. While we understand the feelings of vengeance aroused in Shylock by the indignities he has endured, they do not lodge inside of him as deeply as this because they did not come from his child. Jessica has not only run off with a Christian man, she has stolen his money and jewelry from him and sold a ring of irreplaceable sentimental value to him for a trifle. The shock and pain of this are clear in Shylock's words. He is profoundly wounded in a way that even Antonio could never effect.

This is a vulnerability we can understand and feel. If our loved and trusted daughter betrayed us in this way, we would be overcome with pain, confusion, rage and disbelief and search for some reason to explain it. We would ask: Why did she do this? Did we do something to cause this? Did someone else talk her into it? Who enabled her? How do I find her?

For Shylock all of this grief; the loss of his money, his daughter and his jewelry is the fault of Antonio. The man who has taken his daughter, Lorenzo, is a friend of Bassanio's who is the dear friend of Antonio's. At the same moment that Bassanio departs on a ship, most likely one of Antonio's, Jessica is supposedly in a gondola with Lorenzo. Bassanio's ship is not searched because it has already left port. Is Antonio to be believed when he assures the Duke that Jessica is not on Bassanio's ship?

In Shylock's mind these questions all point to one mastermind: Antonio. It is Antonio who has set all of this in motion and he is the one to blame for this catastrophe. This thought becomes fixed in Shylock's brain and helps us to understand his actions in the famous trial scene. But before we head there we must deal with another aspect of Shylock's nature: His greed.

When Shylock discovers that his daughter has run off with Lorenzo and stolen much of his wealth he is described by Antonio's and Bassanio's friend, Salanio this way:

SALANIO

I never heard a passion so confused,
So strange, outrageous, and so variable,
As the dog Jew did utter in the streets:
"My daughter! Oh, my ducats! Oh, my daughter!
Fled with a Christian! Oh, my Christian ducats!
Justice! The law! My ducats, and my daughter!
A sealed bag, two sealed bags of ducats,
Of double ducats, stolen from me by my daughter!
And jewels, two stones, two rich and precious stones,
Stolen by by daughter! Justice! Find the girl!
She hath the stones upon her, and the ducats!"
-Act II, Sc. viii

It has been often pointed out that Shylock here seems much more concerned for the loss of his money and his jewels than with the loss of his daughter. Is his greed greater than his love for Jessica? We must take into consideration that this description may be an exaggeration colored by Salanio's belief in the stereotype that all Jews are avaricious money grubbers at it must have gotten its fair share of laughs from its Elizabethan audience. But there is also a later passage that comes not from a report about him, but directly from Shylock himself, lamenting to his friend and Jewish compatriot, Tubal.

SHYLOCK

:....A diamond gone, cost me two thousand ducats in Frankfort! The curse never fell upon our nation till now, I never felt it till now. Two thousand ducats in that, and other precious, precious jewels. I would my daughter were dead at

163

my foot, and the jewels in her ear! Would she
were hearsed at my foot, and the ducats in her
coffin!

This is the passage I referred to earlier. Shylock wants
Jessica dead at his feet and in her coffin. Why? So he can
take from her ears the jewels that she stole and recover the
ducats that would lie in her coffin.

This is such a level of craven selfishness and cruel contempt that we recoil from it in horror.

His concerns are not for the safe return of his daughter, but for the recovery of his stolen wealth. His words are
cold-blooded, ruthless and bitter.

We noted before that his words and behavior here result
from his broken heart. That he has been so badly hurt by Jessica's betrayal that he is lashing out with emotions and words
he would otherwise never consider. Nonetheless, this is an
extreme outpouring of vitriol and makes Salanio's portrayal
of him as an avaricious monster seem entirely justified.

But, how well I remember my daughter at a very young
age screaming at me: "I wish you were dead!" when I took
away a favorite toy of hers for misbehavior. She later came
to me sobbing, saying that she didn't really mean it.

We say things in the heat of the moment that we later
deeply regret whether we are eight years old or eighty-eight
years old and they come from existential pain, the kind of
pain that seems to threaten our very existence.

This is what Shylock is experiencing and if we agree
that this is what the moment calls for, we will find it in ourselves. We know that we too have lashed out viscerally, or
at least have *longed* to lash out viscerally, at those who have
caused us intense emotional pain. Here is a place where
that store of feelings can find expression and Shylock needs
them from us in order to express what this all really felt like

to him. He has the right to have his story told truthfully. Let others judge.

There is also a circumstantial reason that Shylock is hit so hard by the loss of his wealth. In both Elizabethan England and in late sixteenth-century Venice very few occupations were open to Jews, money lending being one of the precious few. Shylock's money has been hard earned and amassed over many years. This loss means that it was all for nothing and that he will have to start all over again. But how can he lend what he doesn't have? He will have to turn to the community of other Venetian Jews for their help and build up his business from there. So, Jessica has not only bereft him of his only child, but also badly damaged his livelihood.

The last time we see Shylock is in the trial scene. This is where a judge, in this case Portia, (the woman Bassanio has wooed) in disguise as a man, decides whether or not Shylock is legally allowed to cut a pound of Antonio's flesh from him as the contract between them stipulates.

Attempts are made to dissuade Shylock from this heinous act. Bassanio offers him money and the "judge" pleas for mercy from him. But Shylock is steadfast and refuses them both. He has a sharp blade with him to make the cut and scales to weigh out the pound of flesh. The judge rules that Shylock has the legal right to exact the penalty for Antonio's default.

Will he really do this? It is one thing to make this threat, but it is quite another to carry it out yourself especially in a public setting. How much force will it take to cut through Antonio's breast bone? Does he have the nerve?

Shylock's behavior here can be enacted in many ways. If he has the sheathed knife in his hand from the beginning of the trial this will show the keenness of his intent. If he then takes the knife out when he is given permission by the judge and charges straight towards Antonio, then there is no doubt about his willingness to take this man's life in open court. This is a character who has worked himself into a frenzy of blood-thirstiness and will not hesitate to revenge himself on his enemy. Shylock can legitimately be played and seen this way.

If, however, he has to retrieve the knife from a nearby table and unsheathe it, if he takes a few steps towards Antonio and then a step or two back, all the while gripping and re-gripping his knife, then he has doubts. When the moment actually presents itself this character hesitates. Is there some level at which this Shylock realizes that what he is about to do is wrong? If so, it shows that this Shylock has a conscience. Or is it that he just isn't up to it, doesn't have the stomach for it? Shylock can legitimately be played and seen in all of these ways. But note that each scenario paints a different picture of him: Change the behavior and you alter the perception of the man.

In either case, Shylock does begin his strike at Antonio's heart, but before he can cut into his flesh, the judge stops him.

What is going on in Shylock's mind that allows him commit cold blooded murder? All the slights he endures; the verbal attacks on his greed, his religion and his cultural traditions, the physical abuses to his body, the restrictions placed on him by the society in which he lives, the oath he has sworn to carry this threat through to the end for his people, all of these together still do not seem to me sufficient to set into motion this vile act. No, it is the betrayal and loss of his daughter Jessica that puts the knife in his hand and drives it towards Antonio's heart.

It may seem irrational, but Shylock blames Antonio for the betrayal of his daughter and these kinds of irrational impulses can sometimes rise up, engulf us and activate extreme behavior.

166

Imagine for a moment if Shylock did not blame Antonio for Jessica's actions. Would he still thrust his knife into Antonio's flesh? It is an open question and each actor must find for himself the deepest and most powerful reason for taking Antonio's life in order to fulfill the contractual terms of their agreement.

We have examined Shylock's circumstances and how they have shaped him, parsed the words he uses and tried to understand how he hears the words that are said to him and we have let our discoveries guide us to the feelings and behaviors that belong to him. We rejected our initial attack on his monologue to Antonio in Act I Sc. iii because it violated the long range goal of the character in the scene. We then found a more useful approach to the monologue because it lined up better with the language, thoughts and behaviors of all the characters in the scene. The adjustment worked for the whole scene and not for just a moment or two of it.

Ensouling this character required that some of the more unpleasant facets of our emotional reservoir be drawn out of us so that we could truthfully reflect back outward the feelings and behaviors activated by Shylock's way of thinking about the world and his place in it. And his world is a difficult one to inhabit. But living there is what is asked of us. If we give to Shylock the depth and dimensionality that he deserves, then people will see how it is that life's damage over time can turn a basically good man into a monster.

Characters ask of us that we experience their experiences so that they can feel that we have shown them truly, warts and all. "Yes," they can say, "that is what it felt like to me at that time. Judge me for it as you will, but that was the truth of my experience." We owe them that.

CHAPTER SEVEN

HAMLET, THE TRAGEDY OF HAMLET, PRINCE OF DENMARK

The subtitle of this book is, *Knocking on Hamlet's Door.* This means that we are looking not only for the town or the street where Hamlet lives, but the specific house in where he is to be found, his particular address, his front door. Where is it?

Thousands and thousands of pages have been written about this character. Hamlet is perhaps the most analyzed character in all of dramatic literature. He has even been on the couch with British neurologist and Freudian psychoanalyst Ernest Jones who proposed that Hamlet suffers From an Oedipus Complex. We will examine this provocative idea later in the chapter.

Why the fascination? Partly it is because Shakespeare allows us to enter into this character's innermost thoughts and feelings, into his doubts and struggles, characteristics which make him feel so modern to us. Partly it is because of his extraordinary eloquence, wit and intelligence.

Partly it is because he stands in such contrast to the other, much less complex characters in the play. And partly it is because we think we see so much of Shakespeare himself in the character.

Here is how Shakespearean scholar G. B. Harrison states it in his introduction to *Hamlet* in his edited volume of the complete works of Shakespeare:

"When he wrote it, he was, with all thinking men of his age, in a period of profound disillusionment and pessimism,and made it the vessel into which he poured his thoughts on all kinds of problems: on fathers and children, on sex, on drunkenness, on suicide, on mortality and corruption, on ingratitude and loyalty, on acting, on handwriting even, on fate, on man and the universe. There is more of Shakespeare himself in this play than in any of his others."

This is, of course, speculation, but Harrison makes a good point and our fascination with the character does make us speculate about its creator.

But much of the critical commentary on Hamlet centers around the problem of his "delay."

In Act 1, Sc. v the ghost of Hamlet's father appears before him and tells him that he was murdered by his brother Claudius, Hamlet's uncle, and makes Hamlet swear to him that he will take revenge for this "...foul and most unnatural murder." Hamlet swears to do this and then does not accomplish the deed until the final scene of the play. Why the delay? Why doesn't he plan and carry out the execution of Claudius as quickly as he can?

One train of thought is that he doesn't delay at all. G. B. Harrison believes that this is a non-existent problem.

First, says Harrison, he delays because he has to be certain that the ghost is genuine and not some evil presence tempting him into a murderous and damnable act. Second, he argues, when Hamlet has the opportunity to kill his uncle, he cannot legitimately take advantage of it. Claudius is in prayer when Hamlet comes across him and if Hamlet kills him while Claudius is in a state of grace, then he fears that he will send him to heaven and what kind of revenge would that be?

Finally, Harrison concludes, Hamlet is sent away to England and cannot, therefore, carry out the promised re-

venge until his return. When he is back at the castle in Elsinore Hamlet does kill his father's murderer. The delay is
only circumstantial.

This is a legitimate point of view. Hamlet delays not
because of some flaw in his character, but because when
he has the chance, circumstances prevent it. Bolstering this
argument is the fact that in the very next scene with his
mother, Gertrude, he unhesitatingly thrusts his dagger into a
figure he hears hiding in her room and asks, "Is it the king?"
He has the opportunity and he takes it. There is no hesitation
at all in this moment. In fact, it is quite a reckless act. Unfortunately, the figure he kills is not Claudius, but Ophelia's
father, Polonius.

But, if this is the case, we then have to wonder why
Hamlet takes himself to task so harshly for not acting on his
promise to avenge his father's murder.

In Act II, Sc. ii he cannot understand why an actor can
produce more passion in a fiction than he can produce in
a real life circumstance. When Hamlet asks this player to
recite a favorite passage from a play, the actor weeps and
grows pale when speaking of Queen Hecuba. Hamlet is as-
tonished by this and compares his reactions in real life to the
actor's behavior during the speech:

HAMLET

….What's Hecuba to him or he to Hecuba
That he should weep for her? What would he do
Had he the motive and cue for passion
That I have? He would drown the stage with tears
And cleave the general ear with horrid speech,
Make mad the guilty and appal the free,
Confound the ignorant, and amaze indeed
The very faculties of eyes and ears.

171

Yet I,
A dull and muddy-mettled rascal, peak,
Like John-a-dreams, unpregnant of my cause,
And can say nothing-no not for a King
Upon whose property and most dear life
A damned defeat was made. Am I a coward?
….'Swounds, I should take it. For it cannot be
But I am pigeon-livered and lack gall
To make oppression bitter, or ere this
I should have fatted all the region kites
With this slave's offal.

Here Hamlet condemns himself for being "unpregnant" of his cause, which is to enact his revenge on Claudius. He has done nothing towards this goal. "Pigeon-livered" means he is too soft, too gentle and lacking "gall" means he lacks the spirit to do what he has sworn to do. By now, he laments, he should have fed Claudius's guts (offal) to the birds (kites). But he hasn't.

Hamlet himself is stunned by his hesitancy. An actor's passion is aroused over nothing and yet he cannot awaken a comparable fervor in himself to avenge the murder of his own father. He wants to know what it is that is wrong with him. He has the reason, he has the cause, but he is immobilized. Does this make him a coward, he wonders? Is that his true nature?

In Act IV, Sc. iv Hamlet is on a plain in Denmark and sees an army on the march. When he inquires as to the purpose of this army he is told that it is being led by Fortinbras, the nephew of the Norwegian King, and that this army is on its way to Poland to gain some "little patch of ground that hath in it no profit but the name." Right in front of his eyes Hamlet witnesses men who will risk their lives for a worthless piece of ground. Left alone, Hamlet again berates himself:

HAMLET
How all occasions do inform against me
And spur my dull revenge! What is a man
If his chief good and market of his time
Be but to sleep and feed? A beast, no more.
Sure, He that made us with such large discourse,
Looking before and after, gave us not
That capability and godlike reason
To fust in us unused. Now whether it be
Bestial oblivion, or some craven scruple
Of thinking too precisely on the event-
A thought which, quartered, hath but one part
wisdom
And ever three parts coward-I do not know
Why yet I live to say "This thing's to do,"
Sith I have cause, and will and strength, and
means
To do't.
….How stand I then?
That have a father killed, a mother stained,
Excitements of my reason and my blood And
let all sleep while to my shame I see
The imminent death of twenty thousand men
That for a fantasy and trick of fame
Go to their graves like beds, fight for a plot
Whereon the numbers cannot try the cause,
Which is not tomb enough and continent
To hide the slain? Oh, from this time forth,
My thoughts be bloody or be nothing worth!
                              -Act IV, Sc. iv

Here is an army marching into armed conflict with no compelling reason to motivate them while he, a man with the highest cause for action, stands idly by doing nothing.

Harrison may be right in his view that there is no delay, but Hamlet does not agree with him.

Hamlet simply cannot understand why he does not act, wonders if he is paralyzed by cowardice or by overthinking the issue.

Fortinbras is not the only foil to Hamlet provided by Shakespeare. As soon as Laertes, brother of Ophelia and son to Polonius, learns of his father's death he immediately returns from France, arouses a Danish mob against Claudius believing that he is the cause of his father's death and storms the palace seeking revenge on him. Laertes reacts with blinding speed to the death of his father and takes immediate action.

In contrast Hamlet, faced with the same circumstance, sputters and stalls. Shakespeare has done something new with this character. He has written a revenge tragedy in which with the hero is incapable of acting vengefully.

Now, If the delays are so reasonable, why then is he criticizing himself so scaldingly for them? Shakespeare wants to highlight, not minimize, this delay by presenting two examples of characters who take action quickly and decisively; Laertes and Fortinbras. These characters do not hesitate to do what needs to be done, they just do it. Even the Player can work up more passion about Hecuba than Hamlet can about his own father.

If Harrison is right, then these characters are hardly necessary. Why point up Hamlet's inaction, his lack of motivation, if it doesn't exist? Why give Hamlet two soliloquys in which he upbraids himself for his passivity if delay is not a central theme?

Furthermore, Hamlet is not the only character to comment on his inaction. In Act III, sc. iv, as Hamlet berates and shames his mother for marrying and sharing her bed with Claudius, the ghost of his father makes a reappearance explaining that, "This visitation is but to whet thy almost blunted purpose." Yes, his purpose is indeed blunted and his father's ghost is forced to remind him of his mission and spur him on to action.

In the Player, Laertes and Fortinbras Shakespeare provides three characters who point up Hamlet's passivity and lack of motivation and by having both the title character and the ghost of Hamlet's murdered father note this absence of action in his hero Shakespeare is clearly making it a central issue.

Harrison's view that there is no "delay problem" is peculiar in light of these examples and the attempt to explain it away feels as though it diminishes the complexity of the play and makes of it a more conventional revenge tragedy than it actually is.

If we accept that there is a delay problem in the play, then we can point out an important acting craft note: When a character acts in a way that contradicts their stated objective, it is revelatory of character.

In other words, If Hamlet declares his intention to take revenge on Claudius and then does not do it, we then wonder about his character, we speculate about what it is in him that prevents him from acting on what he says he wants. Perhaps he is too sensitive to commit such a brutal act. Maybe by overthinking, by pondering every angle of an action, he stymies his ability to choose a path. Perhaps he is a new kind of being, a renaissance man who does not believe in blood revenge because it is a barbaric and medieval notion.

This dissonance between what the character desires and how the character consciously or unconsciously subverts that stated desire is profoundly revealing.

Here is a simple example. A man asks a woman to marry him, but then, keeps putting off setting the date for the ceremony. After a while, the woman will soon begin to

wonder if he truly does want to marry her. She will wonder
what is really going on inside of him, wonder if she really
knows this man.

Hamlet's delay makes us wonder what is going on inside of him, makes us wonder if we really know this man.
Who is he? What is his emotional, mental and behavioral
location? What is motivating his character and guiding his
actions?

CIRCUMSTANCES

When we first meet Hamlet he has returned from his
studies at Wittenberg in Germany to attend his father's
funeral in Denmark. (One confusion that crops up is that
Hamlet's father's name is also Hamlet, so, any reference to
King Hamlet is a reference to Prince Hamlet's father.)

King Hamlet's brother, Claudius, has ascended to the
throne and in the less than two months following King
Hamlet's internment has married King Hamlet's widow,
Queen Gertrude, Prince Hamlet's mother. This is hardly a
respectful mourning period for the death of his father. As
Prince Hamlet says to his friend, Horatio, "The funeral
baked meats did coldly furnish forth the marriage tables."

These circumstances would distress anyone. Hamlet's
father dies suddenly from a snake bite and when he returns
home his uncle, a man he strongly dislikes, is crowned king
and then marries his mother.

At this time the Danes chose their king by election of
the nobles and not by the right of succession so Hamlet cannot have expected to be crowned king himself. Unless, of
course, he put himself up as a candidate. Most likely however, he was on his way from Wittenberg to Denmark when
Claudius was elected.

There was some urgency to this election because as

soon as it was understood that King Hamlet had died and that the kingdom of Denmark suddenly had no leader, an army was dispatched from Norway to take back some disputed lands that Denmark had previously won.

If we are to examine his circumstances deeply in an effort to uncover the reason for Hamlet's inability to avenge his father's murder, we must first investigate his relationships with his mother, with Claudius and with his father.

Before he is informed that his father's ghost is mysteriously appearing at the castle in Elsinore, Hamlet expresses his feelings about his father, his mother and his uncle Claudius in a soliloquy from Act I, sc. ii. In it he laments that because of his father's sudden death and the hasty marriage of his mother to his uncle that the world itself has lost all meaning and expresses his wish that he could melt away:

HAMLET

O, that this too too solid flesh would melt,
Thaw, and resolve itself into a dew!
Or that the Everlasting had not fixed
His canon 'gainst self-slaughter! Oh, God, God
How weary, flat, stale and unprofitable
Seem to me all the uses of this world!
Fie on't, ah, fie! 'Tis an unweeded garden,
That grows to seed, things rank and gross in
        nature
Possess it merely. That is should come to this!
But two months dead! Nay, not so much, not
two.
So excellent a King, that was, to this,
Hyperion to a satyr. So loving to my mother
That he might not beteem the winds of
Visit her face too roughly. Heaven and earth!

177

Must I remember! Why, she would hang on him
As if increase of appetite had grown by
By what it fed on. And yet within a month-
Let me not think on on't.-Frailty thy name is
       woman!-
A little month, or ere those shoes were old
With which she followed my father's body,
Like Niobe all tears.-Why she, even she-
A beast that wants discourse of reason
Would have mourned longer-married with my
      uncle,
My father's brother, but no more like my father
Than I to Hercules. Within a month,
Ere yet the salt of most unrighteous tears
Had left the flushing in her galled eye,
She married. Oh most wicked speed, to post
With such dexterity to incestuous sheets!
It is not, nor it cannot come to good.
But break, my heart, for I must hold my tongue!

The world has gone flat and useless and if it was not for religious canon law forbidding suicide, Hamlet would end his life in order to leave it.

His father, whom he compares to the god of the sun (Hyperion), has been replaced by Claudius whom he sees as a lecherous half-man half-goat (satyr). He extolls the care and tenderness that his father showed to his mother not even allowing the wind to blow across her face too harshly. Hamlet makes clear the love and admiration he has for the father he has so recently buried.

His feelings about Claudius are equally clear. His father's brother is as much like his beloved father as he himself is to Hercules. The vast difference he notes between these two brothers reveals the utter contempt that Hamlet

178

feels for the uncle that has married his mother and now sits on the throne of Denmark.

But his most stinging words, his most bitter thoughts and feelings are reserved for his mother.

She is a faithless dissembler. Not two months earlier she acted like she could not get enough of her husband, King Hamlet. She never seemed to tire of her husband, but rather grew more and more in love with him. The more of him she could have, the more of him she wanted ("Increase of appetite had grown by what it fed on.")

But this must have all been for show, an act. How else could she have shaken off the flood of tears she shed at his funeral, recovered from her grief so easily and completely and then remarry within two months of her husband's death? No respectful mourning period is observed and the specter of incest shamelessly ignored.

This is the Denmark to which Hamlet returns. He wants nothing more than to get away from this polluted world and return to his studies in Wittenberg. But his desire is rejected by both the newly crowned King Claudius and by his mother Queen Gertrude. He pointedly tells the Court that he will obey his mother and stay. He says nothing about obeying his detested uncle. Hamlet then refers to Denmark as a "prison" and we can understand why.

But there is one person in whom he can find solace. Hamlet is in love with Ophelia, the daughter of the Lord Chamberlain to the King, Polonius. He has been courting her, giving her tokens of his love and, while away, sending her love letters. He does not seem to acknowledge that he cannot, as a Royal, ever marry her because she is a commoner. She loves him and he loves her and barriers to their feelings are immaterial.

These are the circumstances Hamlet is dealing with at the beginning of the play and they are serious and overwhelming to him. They will only increase in intensity when he learns from his father's ghost that his uncle Claudius, now King of Denmark, is his father's killer.

Before confronting this appalling revelation we have to ask ourselves this: How do we ensoul such extreme circumstances? Especially knowing that they are going to escalate rapidly. Most of us have never experienced anything like the circumstances that Hamlet is exposed to. What facets in us can resonate sympathetically and truthfully with him?

Although we may not have directly experienced anything analogous to Hamlet's situation we all have families. We have a father, a mother, someone we love or have loved. We have loved our parents sometimes and hated them at others. We have sworn our love to someone at some time and sworn at them at some other time. We have also felt betrayed, been deeply wounded by that betrayal and fantasized some form of retaliation against that person or that group at one time or another. It is human.

Maybe you have a step-father or step-mother who tried to act as though they were now your actual father or mother and you resented them all more for assuming this relationship with you.

Even if you haven't, you can imagine it.

Imagine that your mother, who seemed so in love with your father, remarried after his death within two months. What would you think of her? Did she include you in her decision? Explain to you why the mourning period was so short? Hamlet's mother does not seem to have done so.

Hamlet is hurt and surprised by his mother's actions and globalizes his reaction saying,

"Frailty, thy name is woman!" "Frailty" meaning "faithlessness," "fickleness." Have you ever done this? Don't you hear such generalizations all the time? "Men are so dumb!" "Women are so emotional!" "Men are dogs!" "Women are so controlling!" "Men are so controlling!" All the time. We globalize in the heat of the moment even when we know that what we are saying is not true of every man or every woman. We do it anyway. We curse people when they have hurt us and Hamlet is deeply hurt. His mother's behavior has stunned him and he cannot even begin to process it. His beloved father is dead, his mother has betrayed his memory and his hated uncle is King. He is reeling.

It is in Act I, Sc. iv that the Ghost reveals to Hamlet that murder is the true cause of his father's death:

GHOST
….If thou didst ever thy dear father love-

HAMLET
Oh, God!

GHOST
Revenge his foul and most unnatural murder.

HAMLET
Murder!

GHOST
Murder most foul, as in the best it is,
But this most foul, strange and unnatural.

HAMLET
Haste me to know't that I, with wings as
swift
As meditation or the thoughts of love
May sweep to my revenge.

This revelation, that his father has been murdered and not killed by the bite of a poisonous snake, prompts Hamlet

to immediately declare his intention to "sweep" to his revenge. No hesitation.

Next, Hamlet learns the identity of the killer:

> GHOST
> ….But know, thou noble youth
> The serpent that did sting thy father's life
> Now wears his crown.

> HAMLET
> Oh, my prophetic soul!
> My uncle!

His "prophetic soul?" This catches our attention. Hamlet has previously suspected that there was some sort foul play involved in the death of his father and further has entertained the thought that his uncle Claudius was somehow behind it. Now these thoughts are confirmed.

Soon the Ghost departs leaving Hamlet with two words: "Remember me."

Hamlet

Hamlet, already in shock over the sudden death of his father and his mother's remarriage, has this shock redoubled by the appearance of his father's ghost, the disclosure of the murder and the murderer and the charge to avenge it. It is no wonder that when his friends find him just after the Ghost's departure that they find his words "wild and whirling."

How does Hamlet feel about all of this? At the end of this astonishing scene Hamlet says, "Oh, ccurséd spite that ever I was born to set it right."

The oath that he has sworn to avenge his father's death by taking Claudius's life in an act of blood revenge is a curse. What has his beloved father asked of him?

In Act II, Sc. 1, the very next scene after the encounter with the Ghost, Hamlet's behavior is described by a shaken Ophelia to her father, Polonius:

OPHELIA

My lord, as I was sewing in my closet,
Lord Hamlet, with his doublet all unbraced,
No hat upon his head, his stockings fouled,
Ungartered and down-gyved to his ankle,
Pale as his shirt, his knees knocking each other,
And with a look so piteous in purport
As if he had been loosèd out of Hell
To speak of horrors, he comes before me.

POLONIUS

Mad for thy love?

OPHELIA

My lord, I do not know,
But truly I do fear it.

POLONIUS

What said he?

OPHELIA

He took me by the wrist and held me hard.
Then goes to the length of all his arm,
And with his other hand thus o'er his brow,
He falls to such perusal of my face
As he would draw it. Long stayed he so.
At last, a little shaking of my arm,
And thrice his head thus waving up and down,
He raised a sigh so piteous and profound
As it seemed to shatter all his bulk

And end his being. That done, he lets me go.
And with his head over his shoulder turned,
He seemed to find his way without his eyes;
For out o' doors we went without their helps,
And to the last bended their light on me.

This behavior is so revealing. Why is Hamlet behaving in this way?

He has sworn to the Ghost that he will wipe away all memories and thoughts from his mind and will dedicate himself solely to the revenge killing of Claudius. This means he must say goodbye to the woman he loves. His personal feelings for her must be riven from of his heart, wiped away if he is to focus only on his oath. But he cannot simply cast her aside, he must see her one more time. He goes to her private room, disheveled and pale and shaking, saying nothing. He just looks at her as if to fix a final picture of her in his mind before he leaves. A life with her is now impossible and it shatters him. He must let go of her, in more ways than one, and after a few harrowing moments he leaves her room. But even as he does, he cannot take his eyes off of her.

Again we must ask, what has his beloved father asked of him?

After this scene, Hamlet makes two interesting and revealing decisions. First, he decides that he must test the authenticity of the ghost. Maybe the apparition is only impersonating the ghost of his father and could instead be a malevolent spirit tempting him to perform an act that will damn his soul. So he delays until he can prove that the Ghost is genuinely his father's spirit.

Second, he decides to pretend that he is mad and act oddly and strangely around the castle. He does not explain this decision but it is likely that he thinks this will allow Claudius to dismiss him as a fool and, so believing, let his guard down around him. In fact however, this behavior only calls attention to him and makes Claudius wary and suspicious of him. Neither of these strategies helps him to fulfill his sworn oath.

In Act III, Sc. I Hamlet wrestles with his choices in the most famous soliloquy in all of Shakespeare. What is on his mind? How is he thinking? If we are to ensoul him, we must unravel his thoughts and their patterns:

HAMLET
To be, or not to be-that is the question.

Many interpret this question to mean, "Should I live or commit suicide?" This is a reasonable view of these words especially since Hamlet wishes in his very first soliloquy that religious law did sanction self-slaughter. But there is another way to see these words as he seems to restate the question more fully in the next sentence:

HAMLET *(continued)*
Whether it is nobler in the mind to suffer,
The slings and arrows of outrageous fortune,
Or to bear arms against a sea of troubles
And by opposing end them.

If we put this statement together with the opening line, then Hamlet is saying, "Is it better to be the one who quietly suffers the wrongs one is subjected to in life passively, or is it better to be the person who actively fights to end those wrongs? Hamlet is wondering here whether he should let the murderous act of Claudius go, or take up arms against him. Which, he asks himself, is the nobler course? Is he a noble man or is he not? All of us would rather be noble, do the noble thing, and not be the one who is ignoble. It is just as important for Hamlet to see himself this way as it is for us.

HAMLET *(continued)*
>   To die, to sleep-
>   No more, and by a sleep to say we end
>   The heartache and the thousand natural shocks
>   That flesh is heir to. 'Tis a consummation
>   Devoutly to be wished. To die, to sleep-
>   To sleep-perchance to dream. Aye, there's the
>   rub.
>   For in that sleep of death what dreams may
>   come
>   When we have shuffled off this mortal coil
>   Must give us pause. There's the respect
>   That makes calamity of so long life.

If Hamlet takes up arms against Claudius his own death may be the consequence. This is where his thought goes when he says, "To die." And death may not be so bad. After all it is more like being asleep than anything else. Better even. Because heartache and shock disappear forever, the door is barred to them and they cannot enter.

What is Hamlet thinking about when he says heartache? Is it a specific or a general statement? In order to ensoul him, we make it personal. His aches over the malicious murder of his father, over the need to spurn Ophelia, and over the unfathomable betrayal of his mother.

Has he suffered shocks? Certainly all of the above are not only heartaches, but also shocks.

But what shock might Hamlet be recalling here? Being in the presence of his father's ghost.

Here is what he says after the ghost leaves their first scene alone together in Act I, Sc. v:

HAMLET
O all you host of Heaven! O earth! What else?

And shall I couple Hell? Oh, fie! Hold, hold,
    my heart,
And you, my sinews, grow not instant old
But bear me stiffly up. Remember thee!
Aye, thou poor ghost, while memory holds a seat
In this distracted globe.

Seeing his father's ghost causes Hamlet's heart to palpitate wildly, causes his legs to lose their strength and sets his mind whirling. This must be the greatest shock of his life and it assaults him body and soul. The actor might emphasize the word "shocks" here and actually have a subtle bodily reaction as he recalls this chilling incident.

But is it a "natural" shock as Hamlet says in the soliloquy?

In Shakespeare's time the existence of ghosts was accepted by both Catholics and Protestants although they had different ideas about what these entities exactly were. Some believed that they were the actual ghosts of the dead who were consigned to Purgatory and some believed that they were devils posing as the dead tempting the living into various sins. Both of these viewpoints are represented in the play.

Making these heartaches and shocks personal to the experience of the character and not just abstract ruminations, allows the actor an entry point into Hamlet's specific thoughts, memories and feeling life.

Imagine if all of the heartaches and shocks of your life could cease, melt away. Forever. Death offers this.

About two-hundred and eighty-five years after Hamlet debuted on the stage, philosopher Friedrich Nietzsche weighed in on the relief offered by death:

The thought of suicide is a great consolation: by means of it one gets successfully through many a bad night.

So much anxiety is coursing through your body form the stresses of life that you cannot fall asleep; Well, you think to yourself, there is a way out. I could suffer a fatal heart attack sometime tonight, or be in a fatal car accident early tomorrow or take my own life and all of this pain and anguish would cease. Such thoughts can allow a measure of relief to flood your body and loosen the grip of crushing anxiety so that you can finally fall asleep. In the morning you wake up and realize that you have successfully gotten through a very bad night.

Nietzsche specifically references suicide, but Hamlet, in my view, is talking about losing his life in a battle. But it is, as I have said, a valid choice for Hamlet to be considering suicide. In either case, for Hamlet dying is a "consummation devoutly to be wished." I cannot help but hear that word, "devoutly" emphasized with the character's head looking up to Heaven:

"Please, God, make it so," Hamlet seems to be asking, "Get me out of this torment!"

But then a new and logical thought follows. When you sleep you dream. We understand that.

But what happens when you die? No one living knows that. And that is a fearful thing, that is why we live so long and suffer so much and do not end our lives early:

> HAMLET *(continued)*
> For who would bear the whips and scorns of time,
> The oppressor's wrong, the proud man's
> contumely
> The pangs of déspised love, the law's delay,
> The insolence of office and the spurns
> That patient merit of the unworthy takes,
> When he himself might his quietus make
> With a bear bodkin? Who would fardels bear,

> To grunt and sweat under a weary life,
> But that the dread of something after death,
> The undiscovered country from whose bourn
> No traveler returns, puzzles the will,
> And makes us rather bear those ills we have
> Than to fly on to others that we know not of?
> Thus conscience does make cowards of us all,
> And thus the native hue of resolution
> Is sicklied o'er with the pale cast of thought,
> And enterprises of great pitch and moment
> With this regard their currents turn awry
> And lose the name of action.

Fear of the unknown is greater than fear of the known and makes us "rather bear those ills we have than to fly on to others that we know not of." We recognize the truth of this.

Hamlet ask himself a question at the beginning of this soliloquy and now he has his answer.

While it would be nobler to confront and kill the man who murdered his father, he will not take that path because it might lead to his own death and to the unknown consequences that might follow. After all he has heard his father's ghost describe the conditions of his own death in Act I, Sc. v and they are terrifying:

GHOST

> I am thy father's spirit,
> Doomed for a certain term to walk the night
> And for the day confined to fast in fires
> Till the foul crimes done in my days of nature
> Are burnt and purged away. But that I am forbid
> To tell the secrets of my prison house,
> I could a tale unfold whose lightest word
> Would harrow up thy soul, freeze thy young blood,

189

Make thy two eyes, like stars, start from their
    spheres,
Thy knotted and combinéd locks to part
And each particular hair to stand an end
Like quills upon the fretful porpentine.

Because he did not have the rites of the Church and therefore could not cleanse his soul of his sins, Hamlet's father must spend a certain amount of time during the day burning in fire. That is bad enough, but there is more and worse. The Ghost is forbidden from describing the other conditions of his confinement, but he assures his son that if he knew them they would harrow his soul and freeze his blood. This gruesome report cannot be far from Hamlet's mind as he contemplates death whether it be by his own hand or through confrontation.

Now, we need to unravel some of the phrases in this soliloquy. "The oppressor's wrong." In Hamlet's mind the oppressor is Claudius. "The proud man's contumely." This refers to the disrespectful behavior of arrogant people and is less easily attached to a single character in the play. "The pangs of déspised love." This refers to the pain of Ophelia ignoring him and rejecting his love on the orders of her father, Polonius. "The laws delay." Hamlet must wonder in disbelief how Claudius has gotten away with both regicide and fratricide without suffering any consequences. Why hasn't he aroused suspicion, been investigated and found out? Why must this man's punishment fall to him? Where is the law in all of this?

"The insolence of office and the spurns that patient merit of the unworthy takes, when he himself might his quietus make with a bare bodkin?" Here, Hamlet wonders why we patiently put up with insolence from court officials and insults from unworthy people when we could easily make an end to all of it (quietus) with a dagger (bare bodkin)? Polonius and Rosencrantz and Guildenstern come to mind as examples of such people.

Possibly losing his life in the pursuit of his mission is the problem, he concludes. Not because the fear of death is so terrifying, but because the fear of what comes after death is. He comes to the conclusion that his mission is unfulfilled because he fears the consequences of losing his life.

And so, he further concludes that he is a coward and not the noble man he wishes himself to be: "Thus conscience does make cowards of us all." Asked and answered: Hamlet is a coward and so he has lost "the name of action."

When he finally does act, it is in the heat of the moment when "conscience" cannot interfere with instinct and emotion, when he is directly threatened. This is how Polonius is killed. Hamlet feels directly threatened by someone hiding in the room with him and his mother and he strikes.

Now, are we satisfied as actors by Hamlet's conclusion regarding the basic flaw in his nature?

Is cowardice enough to explain his behavior? He accuses himself of it throughout the play.

Psychoanalyst Ernest Jones did not think so. In his 1949 book *Hamlet* and *Oedipus*, Jones explained Hamlet's behavior and delay as a result of Hamlet's Oedipus complex. In essence his argument is this: Hamlet cannot kill his murderous uncle because all Claudius has done is what he himself, unconsciously, wants to do: kill his father and marry his mother.

The idea of the Oedipus complex was first introduced by Sigmund Freud in his 1899 book *The Interpretation of Dream*s and refers to a child's unconscious desire for the opposite sex parent. In a healthy psyche this issue is resolved as the child grows up. But if this does not happen, then the child may develop mild to severe psychological problems. If Hamlet suffers from this condition, Jones maintains, then he must also repress it because it is unacceptable, it is an unthinkable thought and cannot be brought to consciousness.

However, it does help the actor to make sense both of Hamlet's behavior and his inability to satisfactorily identify the cause of his inaction.

This idea was so influential in explaining Hamlet's behavior that Laurence Olivier used it as the basis for his interpretation of the character and it can be seen in his 1948 film of the play.

Nicol Willamson took the idea further in his portrayal of the character and it may be seen in his 1969 film of the play.

Over the decades both this idea of Freud's and its application to Hamlet by Jones have fallen into disfavor because there is scant evidence of the existence of the Oedipus Complex.

But it has opened up the idea that there could be some ambivalent feelings of Hamlet toward his father. In the play Hamlet praises his father several times mostly comparing him to god-like figures. He compares him to the sun god Hyperion and, in a later scene with his mother, Hyperion comes up again and so do Jove, Mars and Mercury. His father has the attributes of all of these gods, Hamlet maintains. And yet he does nothing. Does the man protest too much?

In the Introduction to this book I wrote the following:

"By the end of the term we had learned very little about characterizing.

There were some extraordinary extemporaneous outbursts of genius from the teacher, one nugget of which I will share in the chapter on Hamlet, but no concrete approach to character emerged."

It is time to share this nugget. The teacher was Peter Kass who was on the founding faculty of the new graduate acting program at NYU in 1965 when it opened. One day Kass was talking to us about objectives and obstacles and strategies. He said he would only give this lecture once because he did not like these words. He loved the ideas, but not the vocabulary.

Line objectives he said are what the character wants with every line. Sometimes, he said, a line objective is very simple. For example, the line objective of a question is to get an answer. So ask it like you actually want an answer. A scene objective is what the character wants during the course of any particular scene. A plot objective is what the character wants during the course of the entire play. And then he paused.

Now, he said, we get to the character objective. Let's take Hamlet as an example. Sometimes the plot objective and the character objective are completed simultaneously. If what Hamlet wants is to kill Claudius, then the plot objective for him is the same as the character objective and that is fine because killing Claudius fulfills both. But sometimes, and this is the intriguing part, a character objective can exist outside the boundaries of the play and this can make for some very compelling performances. And sometimes the character objective is not known to the character. In other words, what they really are seeking is hidden from their conscious minds.

For example, you can play the part of Hamlet and have the plot and character objectives end as the play ends. But if you place the character objective outside the boundaries of the play, the audience will sense that there is something more, something driving the character that does not end when the plot does. The audience may not be able to put their finger on it perhaps, but the character will live on in the audience's mind beyond the conclusion of the play itself, because something still feels unresolved.

In Hamlet's case, his character objective is simmering beneath his consciousness and it is this: Hamlet's character objective is to dance on his father's grave.

My mind was reeling. Dancing on your father's grave is a sign of such disrespect, bile and bitterness that I could not see it. Hamlet hates Claudius, not his father. Kass said nothing further about any of this, but I chewed on it for years.

Here now is what I think. Jones' explanation of Hamlet's delay and behavior strikes me as incorrect because I believe Hamlet loves and respects his father as he says he does. He does not want to kill him and sleep with his mother, even unconsciously. This is not what is stopping him.

But, when his father's ghost asks him take revenge on Claudius and to redirect his life to this purpose, something in him shifts.

If we are to ensoul ourselves with a character who is unable to figure himself out, we need to look to the unthinkable thoughts that may be buffeting him or her.

Earlier in this chapter I wrote, "What sacrifices has his beloved father asked of him?"

Honestly, what kind of man asks his son to commit murder on his behalf? Certainly this is the scenario of many revenge plays, but Shakespeare is exploring something different in this play.

He is interested in the effect of seeking vengeance, not in the act itself. And loyal son that he is, a son who worships his father, Hamlet agrees in the moment to this course of action.

Yes, he swears he will do this for his father. He swears to dedicate his life to this cause and to eliminate anything and everything that might distract or deter him from the fulfillment of his sworn oath. But at what cost? Hamlet is not Laertes and he is not Fortinbras. He is not an irrational hothead, but a thoughtful educated and intelligent man thrown suddenly into a bubbling cauldron of deceit, betrayal, murder and incest and who cannot possibly emerge unscathed.

This is the position Hamlet's father has put him in. How

is he supposed to react? How would you react? Hamlet has to kill the King, cruelly reject the love of his life so she will not be a casualty in the dangerous circumstances to follow, and be willing, even eager, to give up his life in the cause. All of this would stop me in my tracks. You? The fact of the matter is, his father's instruction ruins Hamlet's life. All of his plans for a future, vanish as quickly as you can say,

"Revenge his foul and most unnatural murder."

Hamlet delays not because he thinks too much or because he is a coward, but because he if he does what his father asks, it will destroy his life. He tries to motivate himself in moments of torpor, but fails time and again because inside, below the level of consciousness, he is screaming at his father. His hands are folded and he will not come out of his room. He will not budge. His inner self is in full-fledged rebellion.

So, he does little and then, berates himself for doing little. We might well do the same.

And maybe in a feverish dream that he does not, cannot recall, sees himself, after death, dancing and stomping on his father's grave yelling, "Are you satisfied now? You have ruined my life! Is this what you wanted? How could you do this to me, you son of a bitch? Do you have any idea what you have done, how you have destroyed every dream I've ever had?" Why, why, why did you put me in this situation?" Why couldn't you leave it be? I wish you had never come back! If you loved me, you would never have told me, or asked this of me! I hate you!"

It is psychically more tolerable for Hamlet to see himself as a coward than as yet another betrayer of his father. How can he tolerate doing what he condemns in his mother and his uncle?

How can he hate the man he loves and worships? This cognitive dissonance is paralyzing and such thoughts must be driven down from consciousness, they are anathema.

His father was a great man and Hamlet must be a noble son to him and in that way he can differentiate himself from his uncle and his mother. He will not, cannot, replicate their treachery.

And yet, day by day he breaks the oath he has made to his father. Day after day he lets events happen to him. But, few events happen because of him. He reacts but does not act and he is puzzled by his immobility.

This view of Hamlet's delay is human and graspable. When viewed in this way can see how we too might hesitate in Hamlet's situation, our differences from him are now not so distant but closer to us. His dilemma strikes a familiar core in us and activates our feeling life and colors our thoughts and behaviors in ways that Jones' approach does not. It burrows more deeply into our souls than the abstract notions that he suffers from over thinking, or is too sensitive or is too cowardly to engage in vengeful blood lust because these ideas do not address the "why" of his inaction.

How might Kass's character objective manifest in behavior? Hamlet needs to be constantly searching, not coming to conclusions. Even as he says that "…consciousness does make cowards of us all," there might still be some behavior that lets us know that he is not entirely satisfied with this explanation. The actor might make more of the key line, "Oh, curséd spite that ever I was born to set it right," than is usual. It cannot now be a just a rhetorical phrase or a throwaway before an exit. If this is the character objective this line then should be an agonizing insight, executed either with quite subtlety or with bitter exclamation.

There are so many moments in the play, so many lines affected by this character objective that it is impossible to examine them all here. Read the play, or act scenes from it, or approach soliloquys from it with this understanding in mind and see what insights come to you as you do.

Ensouling Hamlet is a tremendous task, both daunting and exhilarating. He requires that many facets of ourselves be available to him. We need to capture his thinking and his thinking patterns in order to truthfully align our emotions and behaviors with his. This triangulating demands of us a deep understanding of his circumstances, demands of us that we see his situation with fresh eyes, as Kass has done, unclouded by received tradition or, perhaps, allows us to refresh that very tradition with our own uniqueness.

Either way, if we have done our work well and entangled our souls with Hamlet's, reflected truthfully back the facets of ourselves activated by the light shed by the character, then when you knock on Hamlet's door he will not only open it for you, he will invite you in.